Ghosts

of Maine

T. M. Gray

4880 Lower Valley Road, Atglen, Pennsylvania 19310

Dedication

With undying love for my children, Tom and Robyn, and for my soul mate, Bob.

Published by Schiffer Publishing Ltd.
4880 Lower Valley Road
Atglen, PA 19310
Phone: (610) 593-1777; Fax: (610) 593-2002
E-mail: Info@schifferbooks.com

For the largest selection of fine reference books on this and related subjects, please visit our web site at
www.schifferbooks.com
We are always looking for people to write books on new and related subjects. If you have an idea for a
book please contact us at the above address.

This book may be purchased from the publisher.
Include $3.95 for shipping.
Please try your bookstore first.
You may write for a free catalog.

In Europe, Schiffer books are distributed by
Bushwood Books
6 Marksbury Ave.
Kew Gardens
Surrey TW9 4JF England
Phone: 44 (0) 20 8392-8585; Fax: 44 (0) 20 8392-9876
E-mail: info@bushwoodbooks.co.uk
Website: www.bushwoodbooks.co.uk
Free postage in the U.K., Europe; air mail at cost.

Other Schiffer Books on Related Subjects
*Schiffer Books has a variety of books relating to ghosts and supernatural phenomena from around the
country. Please visit our website to find topics of interest to you.*

Designed by Mark David Bowyer
Type set in Buffied / Lydian BT / Humanist521 BT

ISBN: 978-0-7643-2827-5
Printed in China

Contents

4   Contents

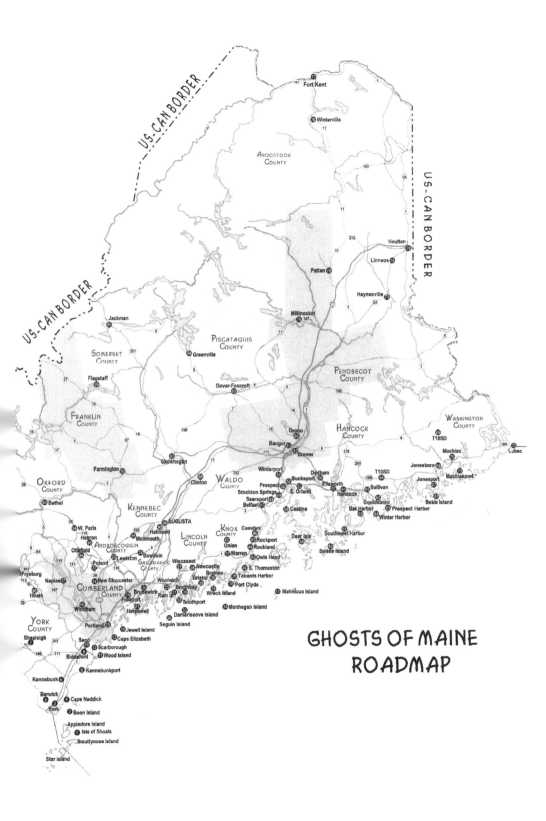

GHOSTS OF MAINE
ROADMAP

Foreword

Unlike my novels, this book is not intended to frighten anyone. *Ghosts of Maine* is a collection of haunted places intended for ghost hunters, although I think anyone interested in Maine history will find this a satisfying, informative read. The state of Maine is home to a vast array of hauntings, and yes, I believe in the existence of ghosts. Perhaps sensitivity to spirits is an inherited ability; my sixth great-grandmother, Mercy Watson Gray, kept hearing what she described as terrible groaning sounds coming from beneath her Brooksville home in the late 1700s. Eventually, a human skeleton was discovered in the cellar (a thighbone thought to be a tree root had served for years as a cellar step). Found with a rusting sword at his side, the remains were thought to be those of a seventeenth century soldier. After re-interment in a proper grave, the noises ceased.

The tendency for clairvoyance may also be an environmental factor as well. My godmother was a full-blooded Micmac lady. She had been born with a caul, a veil of skin attached at the front of her ears covering her nose and mouth. It is said people born with cauls are highly clairvoyant—and she was. My earliest memories are the ghost stories she told: fascinating accounts of strange, otherworldly things she'd experienced and the spirits she'd encountered.

I am not nearly as clairvoyant as Grandmother Gray or my Micmac godmother, but I did see the spirit of my father on two occasions, and have felt the presences of ghosts as well as the sensation of being physically touched by forces unseen more times than I dare count. These encounters weren't scary at all—no more disquieting than an unexpected pat on the back from a friend. Most hauntings, however, are embedded energy called imprints where the ghost doesn't interact at all with changes in the physical environment and takes no notice of the living. This type of phenomenon can be compared to a film that plays on repeatedly.

Ghosts of Maine shows where to find haunted hotspots in places the public is welcome including: roads, bridges, parks, beaches, museums, libraries, forts, lighthouses, restaurants, resorts, hotels, inns, bed-n-breakfasts and cemeteries. Each entry corresponds with a number on the roadmap at the front of the book. Unless you know exactly how to reach your haunted destination, I urge you to navigate by referring to your vehicle's "OnStar" or GPS system (if you have one), a Maine roadmap, DeLorme's Maine Atlas and Gazetteer or any of the online maps showing secondary roads.

One of the reasons Maine is so haunted is due to its history. It became a state in 1820, but the Maine frontier and her islands were settled by Europeans more than two centuries earlier. In the old sailing days, shipwrecks were common tragedies up and down the coast. Maine has its share of phantom ship sightings as well as passengers and crew who never really left the world of the living. Native Americans have lived here several millennia, and many of their oldest stories concern ghosts. In fact, the oldest type of story in the world was probably a ghost story. (One thing I'd like to add here: if I had included hauntings that occur in private homes, schools and hospitals, Ghosts of Maine would have well exceeded a thousand pages ... but because they're often associated with hauntings, I have included curses and ghostly legends, not to mention debunking a few obvious hoaxes.)

Serious ghost hunting calls for knowledge coupled with the caution of an open mind tempered with commonsense, hence for newer ghost hunters, I've included a few guidelines near the end of this book.

Wishing you a safe, successful hunting,
T. M. Gray

Acknowledgments

Maine is home (as well as vacation home) to many writers and storytellers who keep the ghost tales alive. Many of the earliest hauntings would have been lost forever if not for these fine folks keeping track of them. To all those who shared their experiences and stories, I owe a multitude of thanks.

I'd like to thank my husband, Bob, for his constant love and support as well as for the photos he took during our travels together: thank you, darling. Many thanks also go to my sister-in-law, Lora, for helping with not only the enormous task of editing, but for taking several photographs for this book. Thanks are due to her very significant other, Derek, and to my wonderful nephew, Eric. All three accompanied me on various ghost-hunting outings and we always had a good time. Heartfelt gratitude goes also to my father-in-law, Gard, who journeyed with us in Penobscot and Washington counties. I also wish to thank my good friend and soul-sis, Kokie, for her always-valuable insight on this subject and many others.

The Chester County Paranormal Research Society in Pennsylvania supplied the glossary, many heartfelt thanks to them. Thank you, too, Bruce C., for helping me so much with our lady in white, and thanks to Jim F., Pete D., Greg L., Andy S., Patricia and Frank K., Steve B., Richard M., Megan P., my superbly terrific editor, Dinah, Jennifer, and the rest of the Schiffer Books staff, as well as the countless others who've contributed in no small way to the making of this book. I couldn't have done it without you.

Last but not least, I wish to thank the spirits whose stories I've had the honor to pass along. I hope I've done their lives and deaths justice by sharing their histories with my readers.

Disclaimer and Acknowledgment of Trademarks

T. M. Gray and Schiffer Books cannot be held responsible in any way for readers of this book who break the law by trespassing on private property, littering, vandalism or any other crimes. Ghost hunters are responsible for their own actions.

All text (except for the glossary) and all photographs (with exception of the cover photo) in this book are from the collection of the author of this book. This book is not sponsored, endorsed or otherwise affiliated with any of the companies whose names or products are represented herein. They include: "Moxie", the registered trademark belonging to The Monarch Beverage Company, Inc. of Atlanta, Georgia; "Poland Spring Brand Natural Spring Water", the registered trademark belonging to Nestlé Water, North America, Inc. of Red Boiling Springs, Tennessee; "1794 Watchtide", the registered trademark belonging to Patricia and Frank Kulla of Searsport, Maine; and "The Bethel Inn Resort", the registered trademark belonging to Richard D. Rasor.

Ghosts of Maine is wholly derived from the author's independent research including but not limited to newspaper clippings, magazines, books, film documentaries, interviews, phone calls, and emails.

Hallowell, Copyright 2007 by T. M. Gray, first published as "The Hallowell Horror" in QPNTrueCrime, edited by Greg Stephens. Reprinted by permission.

Front and back cover photos courtesy of Bruce Waters, a designer at Schiffer Publishing.

Courtesy of Koko Whitney Berubé.

York County

(1) Isle of Shoals

Seven small islands make up the Isles of Shoals archipelago, located about ten miles off the coast of Maine and New Hampshire. Viking explorers Leif and Thorvald Eriksson may have been the first Europeans to set foot here around the year 1000. In 1605, Samuel Champlain chartered these islands, explored by Captain John Smith nine years later. He called them 'Smith's Isles.' Until a court ruling in 1647, women were not allowed to live there. In 1679/1680, around forty hearty-souled families moved to Star Island in the Isle of Shoals to avoid British taxation. While regarded at the time as heathens by their Puritan peers, the shoalers soon gained respect as successful fishermen.

Star Island is the only island in the Shoals with public access. Star, White and Lunging Islands are part of New Hampshire's waters; Duck, Appledore, Smuttynose, Malaga and Cedar Islands belong to Maine.

In 1715, Star Island was named Gosport after a town near Portsmouth, England. Not long after that, the Isle of Shoals became a haven for pirates: Captain John Quelch, Dixie Bull, Sam 'Black' Bellamy, William Kidd, Andy 'the Scott' Gordon and Edward 'Blackbeard' Teach. Some people thought the pirates buried treasure in various spots in the Shoals.

Some say the Oceanic Hotel on Star Island is haunted with ghosts in its first floor men's room, as well as on the third and fourth floors. These spirits have been heard moving furniture, and opening and closing doors. A woman from Star Island said her daughter-in-law died listening to ghosts scratching for her outside her bedroom window. Betty Moody's Cave on Star Island's east shore, situated between the Breakwater and Lovers' Leap, is where a young mother hid with her infant during an Indian raid in 1689. According to Nathaniel Hawthorne, the cave is formed by "several great rocks being lodged so as to cover one of the fissures which are common along these shores." Poor Betty, either accidentally in fright or perhaps out of desperate necessity, smothered her baby to death. Her phantom wails of sheer despair can still be heard on Star Island usually just before a storm.

Shoals Marine Laboratory, founded in 1973, is located on nearby Appledore Island. The laboratory is an educational research facility. Appledore had been a famous art colony in the 1800s; guests at poet Celia Laughton Thaxter's Appledore Hotel included Nathaniel Hawthorne, Harriet Beecher Stowe, and U.S. President Franklin Pierce. The Appledore Hotel burned down in 1914. Cornell University and the University of New Hampshire run the Shoals Marine Laboratory. The Star Island Corporation owns the island.

On Appledore, people have seen the ghost of a young woman with waist-length blonde hair and beautiful blue eyes overlooking the sea at Golden Girl Point. Some people claim to have heard her murmur "He will come again." This may be the ghost of Mary Ormond, Blackbeard's final common-law wife. Apparently, the pirate left her here on the island in 1718 to look after his buried treasure, but he never returned. In late 1718, near North Carolina's Ocracoke Island, Blackbeard was killed upon capture. (His headless ghost is believed to haunt North Carolina's Pamlico Sound.) Pirate Edward Lowe allegedly killed Mary Ormond in 1722. Others surmise the fair ghost of Appledore may be Martha Gordon, wife of Pirate Andy 'the Scott.' Whoever she is, she still awaits her man's return.

A hog butcher and constable lived in Babb's Cove on Appledore Island in the 1600s. Supposedly, he discovered a large chest in a hole, but, as he tried to lift it, smoke and sulfur caused him to choke and he suffocated. Islanders have seen his ghost—and he's a most disturbing sight; this unfriendly specter is said to appear as a decaying corpse wearing a bloody butcher's apron and brandishing a large knife. Described by Nathaniel Hawthorne in his 1852 journal, Passages from the American Note-Books, and by author Celia Laughton Thaxter, he was so 'desperately wicked when alive' there was no rest for him in the grave. Philip Babb died in 1671 and was thought to have been one of pirate Captain William Kidd's crewmembers—author Charles M. Skinner says Kidd killed Babb so his ghost would frighten away future treasure seekers.

Other Appledore visitors have seen spades and shovels stuck in the ground near Babb's Cove. When they draw near to investigate, the tools vanish. Better phantom tools than meeting up with the ghost of Philip Babb.

Ghosts are said to occupy Smuttynose, an island named for the black 'smutch' of seaweed on its southeast corner, which resembles a nose if you use your imagination. In the winter of 1813, a Spanish ship named the Sagunto wrecked upon Smuttynose's eastern shore. Fifteen unfortunate sailors who made it ashore froze to death in deep snow as they crawled toward shelter. One of Captain Haley's millstones marks their graves. During the winter, their ghosts may be seen on the shore as they wait for a ship to rescue them and take them back to Spain.

A gruesome axe-murder also occurred there. Norwegian sisters-in-law, Karen and Anethe Christensen, were brutally butchered on the night of March 12, 1873. (Karen had worked for the Thaxters on Appledore Island before leaving their employment that February. She planned to spend some time with her married sister, Maren Hontvet on Smuttynose, before leaving to seek employment in Boston.) A big, husky Prussian fisherman named Louis Wagner rowed from Portsmouth to the Isle of Shoals (some say to steal Karen Christensen's severance pay). According to legend, he was in love with one of the Christensen girls, likely beautiful Anethe, who was married to Ivan Christensen. Wagner had lived in the

Hontvet's house on Smuttynose the year before and he knew the family well.

There was no man in the house that fateful night; Maren's husband, John, was out fishing. The door of the Hontvet house was unlocked and the curtains were open. Maren barely escaped being slaughtered—but not before witnessing her sister and sister-in-law's murders. She hid until morning in the rocks on the beach, barefoot and nearly frozen, clad only in her nightdress. Later, Louis Wagner was apprehended in Boston, arrested and put on trial in Saco, Maine. He had taken $15 from the Hontvet house, which he'd spent in Boston on new clothes, a shave, and accommodations the day after the murders. A jury convicted him in less than an hour. He was hung for the murders of the Christensen women in June 1875, the last death sentence ever legally carried out in Maine. In 1904, an old, stained dagger was found hidden beneath the floor in the brick house in Portsmouth where Wagner used to live. Was it his? No one seems to know.

The Christensens were buried at South Cemetery in Portsmouth, New Hampshire. Their murders were the subject of the 2000 movie "The Weight of Water." The axe used as the murder weapon is on display at the Portsmouth Athenaeum.

The Honvet house on Smuttynose burned down a few years after the murders took place, but some say Louis Wagner's ghost haunts those grounds, a woeful spirit full of remorse for killing those he'd called his best friends.

As late as the 1900s, a series of gruesome maimings in the Shoals terrorized certain fishing boats out of Boston manned by Portuguese and Italian fishermen. In those days, such vessels were known as 'Guinea boats.' As the story goes, a drunken crewman of a Guinea boat attempted to rape the wife of a Shoals fisherman and when she resisted, he stabbed her to death. Following the murder, he returned to his ship, which left for Boston the next morning. When the dead woman's husband came home, he found himself blamed for her murder. Facing arrest, the husband escaped in a raging storm, never to be caught. He was seen again, though. One foggy night, the man who murdered the woman was found lying in a pool of blood on the ship's deck; his right hand had been hacked clean off. Several Guinea boats were similarly attacked for almost twenty years thereafter, always on a stormy or foggy night. Faces were mutilated and limbs were chopped off. No one except his unlucky victims saw whoever was doing this. For a long time, Guinea boats stopped fishing the Shoals for fear of the phantom madman. His bloodlust finally sated, the mutilations ceased decades ago; however on foggy nights, more than a few people have spotted a ghostly rowboat manned by a silent sole passenger. Thankfully, it drifts back into the darkness from whence it came.

The Isle of Shoals Steamship Company in Portsmouth, New Hampshire brings visitors to Star Island. For rates, dates and times of departure visit www.isleofshoals.com or call 1-800-441-4620.

---

(2) Boon Island Light

Maine boasts sixty-three lighthouses along its coast, and the tallest lighthouse towering at 137 feet above mean high water is Boon Island Light. This lighthouse can be seen from the mainland on clear days/nights, nine miles off the shores of York. Sohier Park on Nubble Road is a good spot to stop and look … and listen. If you're there on a quiet, windless day, you may hear mournful cries coming from the distant granite lighthouse.

In 1682, the Increase, a trading ship, wrecked upon this island and her four survivors spent a miserable month here, sustaining themselves by eating gull eggs and fish. Their campfire was spotted by Native Americans on Mount Agamenticus who came to their rescue. Some say it is from this incident that Boon Island took its name, but another theory also floats about.

On December 11, 1710, a London merchant ship, the Nottingham Galley, captained by John Dean, ran aground on Boon Island. With no way back to the mainland, no food or firewood save what they could salvage from their broken vessel, ten survivors were eventually forced to resort to cannibalism to stay alive. While no one likes to speak of this taboo, it was sometimes a measure of survival in the old days of sailing. On December 31, the ship's carpenter died; starving crewmen stripped his bones of their "beef" and used the fat from his kidneys to soothe their frostbitten feet. Four days later, a passing vessel discovered and rescued the shipwrecked survivors. Some say it is after this that Boon Island was named—for a long time after, fishermen left provisions on the island (boons, if you will) in case of future shipwrecks. Nine cannons recovered from the water around Boon Island are believed to have been aboard the Nottingham Galley.

In 1799, the first wooden tower on Boon Island was constructed and remained as a lighthouse until a storm on October 8, 1804 destroyed it. A temporary stone beacon replaced it in 1805. Two of its builders drowned in a boating accident as they left the island. A new tower was financed and built in 1812. Nineteen years later, the new tower was demolished by another storm and, in 1852, Congress authorized yet another tower to be built, the same lighthouse that remains on Boon Island to this day.

Records show a heavy turnover in lighthouse keepers on Boon Island since 1855. It's a hard, unforgiving place to live. For one, the island is a barren ledge—the wind and storms here are relentless.

A legend arises from one such storm of a lighthouse keeper who drowned while trying to save his boat. His young bride, Kathleen Brights, pulled him from the rocks and surf, dragging his corpse into the lighthouse, lest his body be swept away. The responsibility of keeping the beacon lit fell solely to her and as the winter storm raged on for days, she went insane. She was eventually rescued, but her mind never recovered from the ordeal.

Lighthouse Mysteries of the North Atlantic by Robert Ellis Cahill describes, "A sad faced young woman shrouded in white," seen on Boon Island by fishermen and Coast Guardsmen. Some claim she is the lighthouse keeper's widow who went insane, her mind and spirit never leaving Boon Island.

Boon's beacon has been reported at times to be mysteriously lit by unseen hands; doors open and close on their own and footsteps have been heard on the stairs. People on the island – as well as boaters in the area – have also reported hearing terrible mournful cries. When the wind is right, the cries may be heard as far away as the mainland.

Currently, the American Lighthouse Foundation owns Boon Island.

(3) Old York Village
140 Lindsay Road, York

Old Witchtrot Road runs north from York Woods Road to Emery's Bridge Road, east of South Berwick. According to author Sarah Orne Jewett, "There is one incident connected with the Salem witchcraft delusion which has given an unforgettable name and association to a certain part of the present town of S. Berwick, in connection with the summoning of Rev. Stephen Burroughs of Wells to appear before the Judges in Danvers." [I believe Miss Jewett meant Rev. George Burroughs, who was accused of witchcraft and executed in Salem on August 19, 1692. Stephen Burroughs was a criminal from New Hampshire in the 1700s.] Two constables sent to fetch Rev. Burroughs found him at his parsonage and, sure of proving his innocence, he agreed to accompany them but suggested they take the shorter path of Old Post Road (Witchtrot Road) through York. On this trip, the constables accused Burroughs of casting a spell upon them, leading them into a gloomy forest and a terrible thunderstorm. They described a diabolical scene where their horses seemed to take flight in the air while lightning flashed and danced around Burroughs. Then suddenly the storm ceased and they found they were near the Quampeagan Brook that flows under present-day Route 236. Today, many people find Witchtrot Road unnerving, the hair standing up on the nape of the neck as if it were indeed haunted.

Sarah Orne Jewett went on to say: "There may have been witches in Berwick: but I never heard of any nearer than York, where one has always been said to lie under a great stone in the churchyard..."

Jewett was speaking of the Old Burying Yard of York and the grave of a "white witch," Mary Miller Nasson, wife of Quarter Master Samuel Nasson. Mary's grave stands out from the others because of the ornately carved headstone and footstone. It's one of the rare old graves that are covered with a slab of heavy stone. Town historians believe it was put there by her husband to prevent pigs from rooting and destroying her grave, however nearby graves from the same period aren't covered with slabs. In a day where families were exclusively responsible for the care and upkeep of their loved ones' graves, Samuel Nasson showed great forethought in placing the stone slab over his wife's grave. After her death he moved from York to Sanford, Maine where he wouldn't have been close enough to properly tend to her gravesite.

Mary Nasson was known as a skilled herbalist and an exorcist in her short lifetime. Since her death on August 18, 1774 at age twenty-nine, her ghost is believed to haunt the cemetery and the area around the Village Museum. It is said that the crows frequenting the cemetery near her gravestone are her "familiars." If you touch the slab covering Mary Nasson's grave, you may detect warmth, especially near the headstone, for there is a discernable temperature difference between the stones. In the not too distant past, children playing near the cemetery told of a kind, invisible lady who played with them and pushed them on the swings; and locals walking near the York Village Historical Museum have seen an apparition of a lady.

Gravesite of York's white witch, Mary Miller Nasson.
Courtesy of Bob Gray.

The Old Burying Yard was actually the second cemetery of York. The graves in it are dated from 1705 through the 1850s. Victims of the Candlemas Day Massacre are also buried in this cemetery in unmarked graves. According to the *Michelin Green Guide*, the Pilgrims of Plymouth set up a trading post at Agamenticus (now York) in 1624 and it became a prospering village. In 1652 it was given the name York by the Massachusetts Bay Colony. In 1692, York fell under a brutal surprise attack by no less than one hundred fifty Wabanaki Natives led by Chief Madockawando on Candlemas Day (February 2).

(As a side note: one of my great-great uncles, Samuel Young, died in this attack along with about fifty of his townsfolk and is likely buried somewhere in this graveyard.)

This terrible massacre no doubt contributed in part to the famous Salem witch-hunt. The devil, colonists believed, was red-skinned, and several of the accusers in the witchcraft trials had extended families wiped out in Indian raids. Cotton Mather spoke of an "army of devils" poised to strike New England, which, according to him, had been "the Devil's land" until the arrival of the Christian colonists.

The Old Gaol in York is the oldest Colonial public building in Maine. It was constructed in 1719 from the timbers of the royal prison built at Meetinghouse Creek in 1656. In 1900, it became a museum in Old York Village. The jailer's quarters and cells are preserved to remain just as they were in the Colonial era. One of the displays at the Old Gaol is The Pirate's Bible or The Old Trickey Bible that some claim is a haunted object.

The bible had belonged to Francis Trickey, a fisherman and former sea captain of reclusive, cantankerous temperament who lived in York in the 1650s. Shortly after Trickey's arrival, cattle belonging to his neighbors sickened and died; the following year, crops failed miserably and people began to whisper accusations of witchcraft. Naturally, Trickey drew suspicion, as his neighbors had witnessed bizarre behavior from him. No one understood why he made circles in the sand with coils of rope, but in Puritan thinking, certainly no good could come from it. Several men began to follow him on his solitary walks into the woods. Was he there to converse with the devil, or perhaps to guard over a secret stash of pirate loot? The answer was never known—Francis Trickey died in the woods, frozen to death during a blizzard, and upon his death the settlers enjoyed an immediate reversal of luck. According to local folklore, when Trickey died, his soul was eternally punished to loop mounds of sand by rope at Bra'boat (Braveboat) Harbor. On stormy nights, his ghost can be heard at Cape Neddick crying for more rope. In the York museum, people examining Trickey's Bible have seen it suddenly slam shut on its own. They claim it won't stay open—sometimes it even snaps shut in people's hands.

Massacre site, Old York Burying Yard.

In 1719, Patience Boston, a pregnant Native American woman, was sentenced for the drowning murder of a reverend's son as well as attempted murder of the reverend and his wife by poison. Patience was jailed on the second floor of the Old Gaol until she gave birth, then she was hanged at Stage Neck. Many believe her ghost is searching for her baby and haunts the Old Gaol; in the past, several museum workers have refused to be alone there.

Like the Old Gaol, the Emerson-Wilcox House is part of the York Village Museum. It was built by George Ingraham in 1742; its last addition was added in 1817. Here visitors can experience what a Colonial home was like. One of its pieces is the tea table belonging to Rev. Joseph Moody. (Nathaniel Hawthorne's 'The Minister's Black Veil' was inspired by this man. At age eight, Moody had accidentally shot and killed his best friend, the 12-year-old son of Captain Anthony Preble. For this, he bored the heavy weight of guilt the rest of his life, finally confessing on his deathbed in 1753 that he, not Indians, had killed his friend.) Throughout his life, he'd been haunted by the specter of his childhood friend, a ghost boy with a hole in his temple. Legend says that after Moody's wife died in childbirth, the rest of his children were taken away for Moody was considered an insane and unfit father. He supposedly penned a journal with obscene and Satanic verses, but historians favor the opinion that Moody suffered a nervous breakdown after the church took his house away from him.

The Emerson-Wilcox House exhibits samples of the only Colonial American crewelwork (a form of needlepoint) known to survive from the 1700s. Visitors have reported seeing the ghost of a bride lying on a bed. She has also been seen standing at the top of the stairs. Apparently, the ghost bride is more active in the fall as the museum shuts the houses down for the winter. She is especially apparent to children and animals.

Old York Village's Research Library and administration office are open year round. The Museum buildings are open to the public June through Columbus Day weekend, Monday through Saturday from

10 a.m. to 5 p.m. Some buildings have limited handicap accessibility. Admission fees with group and senior discounts. Children under age four get in free. For more information, visit the Old York Historical Society at: www.oldyork.org or call 207-363-4974.

The Orchard Farm Tavern on Route 1 in York is home to the ghost of a little girl with long blonde hair, as well as the spirit of an ill-tempered man. Over the years, visitors have reported shifting cold spots, visual manifestations, and disembodied voices laughing and crying.

To get to Mount Agamenticus from Route 1 in York take Mountain Road to Summit Road. If you decide to hike to the top, on a clear day ... you'll be treated to awesome panorama: the White Mountains to the northwest, the skyscrapers of Boston to the south—but before you leave, be sure to pay tribute to the spirit of Saint Aspinquid. The story of Aspinquid's death may have been fashioned from that of an early Eighteenth Century Sokosis Chieftain named Chocorua. According to historian John Joycelin, Chief Chocorua flung himself from a mountain to save his scalp from being taken by the English. The legend on the plaque at Mount Agamenticus tells of settlers chasing St. Aspinquid when he jumped from the west face of the mountain and plunged to his death. His funeral was fashioned after that of Chief Passaconaway and attended by tribal members from near and far who brought gifts of animal skins and meat. A large rock pile near the parking lot stands as a memorial to St. Aspinquid, and anyone who pays tribute to his soul by placing a rock on his grave is assured of having favorable luck in the future.

(4) Cape Neddick

On Nov 30, 1842, the barque ship Isidore, piloted by Captain Leander Foss, set sail for New Orleans, Louisiana from Kennebunkport, Maine with a crew of fifteen. Sailor Thomas King had a bad premonition about the voyage, as did another crewman, who said he'd dreamed of seeing seven coffins, his own included. When the witch of November came calling with blinding snow and gale winds just twelve hours after the Isidore launched, her main mast snapped. Foundering out of control, she ran aground at Bald Head Cliff, just north of the Nubble at Cape Neddick in York, Maine. The next morning, the bodies of seven frozen crewmen were found, the rest were lost to the Atlantic. One body found was that of the Isidore's cabin boy, George P. Lewis, who was only fifteen. He is buried in Kennebunkport. His crewmates, including the man who dreamed of coffins, are believed to be buried near him in unmarked graves.

On cold, stormy nights, the Isidore may still be seen sailing near Cape Neddick Light, which was commissioned in 1874. This ghost ship is said to possess a pleasant spirit, which brings tranquility to those in distress. Throughout the years, the Isidore has been spotted along the coast in Rye and Portsmouth, New Hampshire and in Portland and York, Maine, and is memorialized in the 2001 Harvey Reid song, 'The Wreck of the Isidore.'

(5) Crest Hill, Berwick

Ezra Crowley (name changed) lived on a farm in Crest Hill (name of hill changed) in Berwick, Maine in the mid-1700s. He was exceedingly cruel when he drank and he drank often at the Berwick Tavern. His sons all ran away from home in their early teens, leaving their three sisters: Sadie, Mollie and Annie as virtual slaves on the Crowley farm. In an era where women had few rights, these girls weren't allowed to attend school, but Ezra did let them go to church occasionally. If he discovered that his girls had so much as spoken to a boy, he'd beat them so severely that they wouldn't be allowed out in public until their bruises faded.

One day, Annie, the youngest, asked if she and her sisters could go to Berwick's annual harvest dance. None of them had ever been to a dance before. Ezra adamantly refused but not before slapping Annie back into complacency. After their father left for the town pub, the three girls decided to go to the dance anyway. They had planned to be back home long before their father finished drinking at the pub.

The Crowley sisters weren't in church the next morning. That wasn't unusual, but after a month passed and they weren't seen anywhere, the boys they'd danced with began to worry. They went to Crest Hill to check and see if the girls were okay. In the moonlight, they saw the sisters dancing and laughing in a clearing and they called out to them, but the girls ran away. Thinking that perhaps Ezra was nearby, the boys went home.

When asked about his daughters in the months to come, Ezra claimed they were busy working on the farm, but years later Mrs. Crowley's deathbed confession revealed that Ezra had caught his daughters coming home from the forbidden dance—and had executed the girls by hanging them one by one from the rafters in his barn.

A road crew discovered the remains of the murdered girls decades later when Birchwood Lane was constructed. The sisters were given proper Christian burials in the Evergreen Cemetery on Pine Hill, but on every full moon in September, locals claim the sisters can be seen and heard dancing and laughing in the place that used to be called Crest Hill.

(6) The Kennebunk Inn
45 Main Street, Kennebunk

This inn was built as a private home in 1791 for Phineas Cole; he sold it in 1804, and from there it had several changes of ownership. In the late 1920s, it became an inn called 'The Tavern.' In 1940, Walter Day expanded The Tavern to sixteen guest rooms and re-named it 'The Kennebunk Inn.' In 1980, Arthur LeBlanc purchased the inn and six more rooms were added. He found it a bit odd that a set of stairs in the cellar led to the ceiling and stopped.

Arthur LeBlanc, a retired Air Force officer, discovered the inn was haunted during its restoration. He'd heard noises in the cellar, felt unexplainable drafts in the barroom, where sometimes he'd find bottles tipped over and spilled—after he'd cleaned up. A housekeeper reported feeling a cold gust of air. A couple from Nashville, Tennessee had stayed in Room 104 and said that they had heard knocking on a wall during the night. A maintenance man who'd been working at the Kennebunk Inn for fifteen years came in to check the boiler and heard footsteps on the cellar stairs but saw no one. One waitress was so frightened by something in the cellar that she ran out screaming and never returned.

Cyrus was the nickname a waitress gave the ghost said to haunt the area near the cellar stairs. Evidently, he's the kind of spirit that likes to wander a bit and cause mischief from time to time: several customers have witnessed waitresses carrying trays of stemware when a glass in the middle would leave the tray and levitate slowly upward, then crash to the floor. On another occasion, several customers witnessed as a hand-carved German stein flew from a shelf behind the bar and struck the bartender on his head. No one was seen standing near the shelf at the time. When Jon Towle was bartender, he would tell of a firebox that suddenly flew about twenty feet from its post on an opposite wall.

According to historic writer, Robert Ellis Cahill, he, the LeBlancs and several friends were at the bar discussing the haunting when an elderly stranger asked if Cyrus still worked there. When told that Cyrus was their resident ghost, the old gent said he had stayed in a room at the inn before World War II and Cyrus was the night clerk back then. Not surprisingly, his desk had been in a room directly behind the bar and right above the unfinished cellar stairs.

(7) Bryant's Hollow, Shapleigh

In 1801, Reverend Bryant of Ossippee worked as a traveling retailer, selling pots, pans, and small household items as well as medical goods. On horseback, he traveled several days a week to various Baptist churches in York County, selling and trading goods along the way. A regular rest stop for the Reverend was Joseph Hasty's Inn in the town of Shapleigh. One fateful morning, this would be the last time anyone saw him alive.

The next Sunday, a small but faithful congregation waited for Reverend Bryant to arrive at Deacon Hill's home. As evening fell, the rider who had been sent to fetch the Reverend came back with worrying news of the man's disappearance. The Bryant family was dreadfully apprehensive, especially after the Reverend's horse returned to the barn without him.

Suspicions soon pointed to Joseph Hasty, owner of the inn, the last known location of Reverend Bryant, especially after Mrs. Hasty found clothes belonging to the Reverend tucked in the back of a closet in her home. Unable to say what had become of the clothes, she was later seen with a black eye.

Travelers passing through Bryant's Hollow, where Reverend Bryant disappeared, have come to believe the area is haunted. Some have been thrown to the ground as their horses shied away from something they could not see. Others felt the hair stand up on the napes of their necks as if someone was watching them. Had Reverend Bryant met his end in this place? Had he been killed by Indians or mauled to death by a bear? Everyone suspected some kind of terrible fate had befallen him.

At dusk, a young traveler was confronted in Bryant's Hollow by a man on foot dressed in grey who asked for help. The young man recognized Reverend Bryant at once. He said he'd been murdered by a thief named Warren—and Joseph Hasty, owner of the inn, had helped his killer. Bryant's ghost gestured toward a big oak tree and the young man noticed the letter 'B' carved into its bark. This was where, according to the ghost, his remains were buried. This spirit would not rest in peace until he received a proper Christian burial.

The young man returned to look for the oak in Bryant's Hollow, to show others where the Reverend's body was buried, but he could never again find the tree with the letter 'B' carved in its trunk. Hence, the grey ghost of Reverend Bryant still walks the woods of Shapleigh.

(8) Kennebunkport

The Tides Inn By-The-Sea
252 King's Highway
www.tidesinnbythesea.com

The Tides Inn By-The-Sea, a shingle-style Victorian mansion on Kennebunkport's Goose Rocks Beach, was originally built as the New Belvedere Inn in 1899 by architect John Calvin Stevens for owner Emma Foss. Over the years, the inn has had its share of famous guests including Sherlock Holmes creator Sir Arthur Conan Doyle, President Teddy Roosevelt and acclaimed actor John Hurt who has starred in many movies including 'Rob Roy,' 'Alien,' and 'The Elephant Man.'

According to the inn's current owner, Marie Henricksen, who purchased it in 1972 and runs it with her daughter Kristin Blomberg, the ghost of Emma Foss lets them know if she approves or disapproves of renovations made to the inn. Marie knew almost immediately that her inn was haunted: one of the first signs was the fire alarm going off for no reason at night near Room 25, which was Emma's bedroom. Beds shaking and guests being tucked in for the night by unseen hands and an apparition of a middle-aged woman have been reported over the years. In Room 29, painters were startled to see a female specter in a blue and white striped dress leaning by the door watching them. The mural they painted on the wall of the staircase includes the ghostly image they saw.

Emma doesn't appear to like men named Allen, and not without good reason. She had to sell her inn to the desk clerk, a man named Mr. Allen, so if you stay here, you may catch a glimpse of Emma in her rocking chair on the upper porch. If your first or last name is Allen, you can probably count on something supernatural occurring, especially if you book your stay in Room 25.

Nonantum Resort
95 Ocean Avenue

Kennebunk is an ancient Wabanaki word meaning 'Long Cut Bank'; it describes the peninsula at the mouth of the Mousam River. Kennebunk's first settlement was Cape Porpoise, established in 1610. Centuries later, Summer Street in Kennebunk became Maine's first National Register Historic District.

The original inn that later became the Nonantum Resort opened on July 4, 1884. It is one of only two remaining inns from that era in Kennebunk. The inn began with twenty-eight rooms and ten staff members. In 1930, the rear wing was added. In 1973, the front Wicker Wing was built, and the Portside Lodge was added in 1987. At present, the Nonantum Resort has one hundred fifteen guest rooms and one hundred twenty-five staff.

Tina Hewett, the Nonantum Resort's general manager, said in *MaineToday*, "Former guests and employees still walking the halls bring in a few paying customers looking for more than a comfortable room." Although the Nonantum Resort isn't advertised as haunted per se, some guests come here in hopes of a paranormal experience

... or perhaps a glimpse of Sadie, one of the ghosts that are said to roam the halls. The spirits at the Nonantum are very friendly and have never caused any harm.

According to Hewett, the ghosts tend to "get a little more restless" when the Nonantum is shutting down for the winter, so perhaps that would be the best time to reserve a room and see a ghost.

Captain Lord Mansion
6 Pleasant Street

Designed by architect Thomas Eaton, this stately Federal-style home was built during the War of 1812 by Captain Nathaniel Lord, a shipbuilder and merchant. Back then, Kennebunkport was part of the town of Arundel. Most of its rooms are named after ships built by Captain Lord. He died the year the house was completed. The mansion remained in the Lord family for the next one hundred fifty plus years. Lord descendant Charles P. Clark did extensive renovations, which were blueprinted by William Ralph Emerson, in the late 1890s. Sally, Charles' daughter, and her husband Edward Buckland, used the mansion as a summer home until Sally's death in 1941. She is fondly referred to as the "ghost of the house." The Bucklands' daughter Julia owned the mansion after her mother's death, but sold it in 1972 to a speculator who turned it into a boarding house for elderly women. It was resold in 1978 and became a bed and breakfast.

In the late 1970s, while being lovingly restored to its former glory, and despite open windows, a stench like that of rotting fish was suffered by the workers—the smell disappeared as soon as the renovations were finished. A portrait above the fireplace in the Music Room depicting Lord descendant Sally (Clark) Buckland sometimes appears to glow. Radios switch on and off by themselves, footsteps have been heard in several rooms throughout the mansion, traveling through walls, and sometimes accompanied by moving lights and orbs.

In the Lincoln Room, the ghost of a young woman thought to be Phebe Lord, Captain Lord's widow, dressed in early 1800s style clothes, has been seen by at least two witnesses on separate occasions rocking in a chair that floated across the room. The woman appeared to age rapidly before disappearing. The Lincoln Room was originally the Wisteria Room, meaning a remembrance of the dead. She has also been seen on the spiral stairs leading to the octagonal cupola. Phebe's Fantasy, a small four-bedroom inn dating back to 1807, can be found directly behind the Captain Lord Mansion.

The Captain Lord Mansion is listed on the National Register of Historical Places.

(9) Biddeford City Theater
205 Main Street, Biddeford

As seasoned ghost hunters know, theaters, opera and playhouses tend to attract spirits that are drawn to emotional energy. Sometimes they are haunted by previous owners or people who worked there ... and in some cases, past performers visit them.

The old Opera House City Theater near Biddeford City Hall is one such case. It was built in 1860 and its first performance was a play about slavery. The theater was rebuilt by Maine architect John Calvin Stevens in 1896 after fire destroyed it on December 31, 1894. Along with local acts, it has also hosted live performances by greats such as Fred Astaire, Mae West, W.C. Fields and Laurel & Hardy ... but the "un-live" acts make it a paranormal hotspot.

On Halloween night in 1904, lovely 31-year-old opera soprano, Eva Gray of the Dot Karroll Repertoire Company of New York, sang her last song on this stage. After her third encore, a song titled Good-bye, Little Girl, Good-bye, Eva left the stage, collapsed in her dressing room and died from a heart attack an hour later, leaving her beloved husband and their 3-year-old daughter. Patrons, performers, technicians and others swear that ever since her death, Eva Gray has haunted this theater. She is said to show approval of present-day performers by swinging the overhead lights. According to a technical director, lights in a dressing room flicker on and off, despite electrical breakers being in the off position at the time. A spokeswoman for a Maine senator was performing solo in 1986 and claims she heard the overhead work lights shake and move. No one was up there at the time. Sometimes Eva's sweet voice can be heard singing or whispering softly, along with the sounds of her footsteps. Students have witnessed her silhouette hovering near the restrooms and many have felt unexplainable cold spots. (According to one choreographer-actress, "You could always tell when she [Eva] was around because the air was very cold.") A bright

Eva Gray's ghost sings at the Biddeford City Theater.

orb of light has been spotted drifting across the upper balcony of the theater, but Eva is not the only ghost on the premises ... one technical director said some people have heard the disembodied voice of a young girl backstage, calling for her mother. Could it be Eva's little daughter?

The other ghost, known as Mr. Murphy, was an arc-light projectionist in the 1930s and 40s when the theater was showing movies. He's still on the job some say, nervous as ever when the switches on the electrical breakers are flipped ... especially if a woman is doing it. In life, he didn't want ladies touching the electrical equipment—and apparently he still doesn't. During a teaching session, a group of schoolchildren and the theater's creative director witnessed an aluminum ladder shaking on its own as if being climbed. Names have been shouted when no one is there to do the shouting. Ghosts seem content to visit this theater from time to time and while their presences may be startling, they're never out to frighten anyone. Biddeford City Theatre is a wondrous old building and the people who work there love their ghosts.

(10) Saco River

A headline in a 1947 *Maine Sunday Telegram* read: "Saco River Outlives Indian Curse." Apparently, it was the first time anyone could remember that three lives had not been lost in the river.

For centuries, many people in Saco considered the river to be cursed by a powerful shaman, Chief Squando of the Sokokis Tribe, whose summer home was on Indian Island (now Factory Island in Saco). Chief Squando, his wife Awagimiska and their little son Mikoudou lived in peace with the English settlers, who were friendly and willing to trade goods. Chief Squando was said to have returned a white girl captured years earlier in a raid, and during the first part of King Philip's War, he remained benevolent toward the white settlers.

Then came a fateful day in 1675 when three sailors off an English vessel anchored near Cow Island drowned the chief's infant son,

Mikoudou. They wanted to see if little Indian babies could swim like beavers. (John Jocelyn, who wrote the first narrative of a journey up the Saco River, New England Rarities Discovered, described this tragedy in his notes.) They rowed up beside Awagimiska's canoe, seized the infant from his mother, and cruelly tossed him into the water. Awagimiska, pregnant at the time, jumped in to rescue her son. Her frantic fingers caught his blanket, but the river tore him away from her, then it took her life and that of her unborn child as well.

Chief Squando was as outraged and heartbroken over the deaths of his family. It is said he "wrought a spell with his fire smoke, his blown-up bladder skins with their rattling peas inside, and his strange-smelling herbs." Then he waded knee-deep to the place where his wife's empty canoe had come ashore. Here he chanted and poured "bad medicine" into the river, summoning the evil Hobowocko, and cursing the river so that as long as white man lived by the river, three of his race must drown in it every year.

The first major battle in King Philip's War was fought in Saco and was likely initiated in part by Chief Squando. Eventually the chief made peace once more with the settlers, but Hobowocko's power proved too strong and neither he nor the medicine man were unable (or unwilling) to lift the spell. By 1947, the curse finally ended. Though almost every year someone drowns in the Saco River.

(11) Wood Island Light

Built in 1808, the octagonal wooden lighthouse was replaced in 1839 by a 38-foot granite tower and was renovated in 1858 to allow for another lens. Eben Emerson served as lighthouse keeper during the 1860s. On March 16, 1865, he saved the crew of the British brig Edyth Anne from drowning in a heavy storm. Then, Captain Thomas Henry Orcutt served as keeper of Wood Island Light for nineteen years (1886-1905). His dog, Sailor, became quite famous at the time for ringing the station's fog bell for passing ships by pulling the bell cord with his teeth.

Wood Island is located just offshore from the Biddeford Pool. (The Pool is considered by some to be a miracle pond, as those who bathe there on the twenty-sixth day of June are supposedly restored to full health. June 26 is feast day of at least sixteen saints.)

Wood Island was also the site of a grisly murder-suicide. Twenty-four-year-old Howard Hobbs was a part-time lobsterman living on the west end of the island. On June 1, 1896, Hobbs was drunk and late on his rent. When game warden Frederick W. Milliken, who also lived on Wood Island with his wife and children, asked Hobbs if the gun he carried was loaded, Hobbs shot him in the chest.

Milliken's wife tried to take the gun away from him and he threatened to shoot her as well, but was talked out of doing so by the dying man. Mrs. Milliken then convinced Hobbs to turn himself in to lighthouse keeper Captain Orcutt, who hurried to the bedside of Milliken and witnessed his death at 5:15 that afternoon. When Hobbs learned of Milliken's death, he told the grieving widow that he was going home to shoot himself in the right temple. He went to his cottage and moments later, the Milliken family heard a shot ring out. Hobb's friend, Will Moses, found his body on his bed, gun at his side, muzzle near the pillow and a bullet lodged in a roof timber. Hobbs left a letter for a girlfriend and a note for Moses on the table. Some claim Howard Hobb's ghost still haunts the island; witnesses tell of doors banging shut, window shades that raise and lower on their own, and the eerie echo of a gunshot.

Photographs in the basement of the Wood Island Lighthouse were taken by (NEGP) New England Ghost Project members who visited the island in 2005.

Wood Island Light can be seen from just beyond the southern end of Route 208 off the Biddeford Pool. For the best viewing spot, take Lester B. Orcutt Boulevard off Route 208. An entrance to the East Point Sanctuary Audubon Trail on the left side of the road leads to the ocean. Wood Island Light is directly across the channel. Friends of Wood Island Lighthouse run seasonal tours to the island and lighthouse from Biddeford Pool.

Cumberland County

(12) Scarborough

Garrison Cove, Ferry Place, Prouts Neck, and Scarborough

Centuries ago, a ferryman worked the Owascoag (Scarborough) River, and on one raging, stormy night, he heard the voice of a stranded man on Blue Point, begging to be ferried across the tumultuous waters. "Cross the river as you will, an' you may go to the devil if you will, but I'll not put over the stream this night!" the ferryman shouted back. The next morning, he found the drowned corpse of the man who'd called for help. His ghost has been paying penance ever since, for during storms, the ferryman may be seen shouting, "Go to the devil!" against gale winds as he pushes his boat across the river, the specter of a dank corpse at his feet. When the storm is over, the ferryman, his boat and his passenger, fade into the mist.

Garrison Cove is located on the western side of Prouts Neck near the Bird Sanctuary.

Massacre Pond
416 Black Point Road

On Prouts Neck just behind Scarborough Beach Park, there's a freshwater pond formed from a salt-water tidal lagoon. This is Massacre Pond, the site of two Native attacks on settlers. The first occurred in 1677 when forty settlers died after being ambushed. The second attack happened in 1703 (the plaque there says 1713).

In his early twenties, Richard Hunnewell lost his family when a band of Abenakis randomly attacked his small farm on Black River. He came home to find his young wife murdered and scalped and their baby son's brains were bashed out inside their cabin. (Usually women and children were taken alive to be traded back to the English settlers for money or supplies—or they were sold as slaves among tribes as far north as Canada.) The frenzied attack on Hunnewell's family was unusually gruesome. He vowed to avenge his family by killing every Native American he could find; not long after the attack he left his farm and became an "Indian fighter."

By 1697, the weary Indian fighter returned home to Black Point, his body bent and ravaged with battle scars. His nickname 'Crazy Eye,' may have been due to an injury, but was more likely given because he tended to shoot randomly in the midst of battle. The General Court granted Hunnewell monetary assistance because of his disabilities. On October 6, 1703, he was tending cattle with nineteen other men when they walked into an ambush by over two hundred Abenakis from Canada. Hunnewell was the only settler armed with a gun. Some of the Abenakis likely recognized the old Indian fighter with the crazy eye, and remembered how he seemed to live for killing their people. At the end of this massacre, Richard Hunnewell was among the dead, his arms severed, an arrow running through his thigh. What could be found of his remains were buried near the pond where he died.

Tales of Hunnewell's ghost go back three centuries; even today, people are still seeing the specter of the old Indian fighter at the pond. They describe him as he was when he died, horribly maimed and bloody, always recognizable by his crazy eye.

Massacre Pond is at Scarborough Beach State Park and is open to the public during daylight hours. Admission is $4 per person. A footbridge spans the pond and leads to a beautiful sandy beach at the mouth of Saco Bay.

Massacre Pond at Scarborough Beach State Park.

(13) Cape Elizabeth

Inn By The Sea
40 Bowery Beach Road
www.innbythesea.com

Twenty-one-year-old Lydia Carver was one of seven children of Amos Carver, a Freeport businessman. In early July 1807, she sailed to Boston to have her trousseau, her bridal dress and its petticoats, fitted. No doubt, she was excited about her upcoming wedding and anxious to return home.

Lydia boarded the schooner Charles on Sunday, July 12, with twenty-one other passengers for the overnight voyage from Boston to Portland. One of the passengers was the wife of the schooner's Captain, Jacob Adams of Portland. The Charles cargo was valued at $25,000.

All seemed to go well; the seas were calm and the winds light as they left Boston Harbor, but as they approached Portland, a storm suddenly struck, and just before midnight, fog settled in. As the Charles neared Richmond's Island (formerly known by mariners as The Isle of Bacchus), its hull struck the jagged rocks of Watt's Ledge. The Charles rolled over on its side, water pouring in. Four men, including Captain Adams, tried to swim the seventeen or so yards to Richmond's Island, but the good captain turned back when he heard the screams of his wife as the ship continued to sink. He was carried out to sea before he could reach her.

The sea-battered body of Captain Jacob Adams was found the next day. He was buried in Portland's Eastern Point Cemetery.

Six passengers who managed to cling to the foundering ship through the night were rescued around 9 a.m. on July 1, 1807; the rest had been wrenched away from the wreckage and drowned. Most of them are buried in the small graveyard next to the Inn By The Sea, not far from the shore where their bodies were found. Lovely Lydia Carver was found next to the trunk containing her recently fitted bridal dress. She, too, rests in the graveyard, but the same cannot be said of her spirit, which haunts the Inn By The Sea.

According to staff at the Inn, the lobby elevator ascends to the second floor late at night. It comes back down, but no one is inside. Tables set for breakfast have been re-arranged, cups, plates and silverware piled atop one another. A dining room manager witnessed a metal cash box fly across the room from its kitchen shelf. The executive housekeeper, getting ready to leave for the night, would see lights turn on in rooms where she'd just turned them off, and guests have told the front desk manager that someone has been in their rooms ... and yet they've seen no one there. A former manager of the Inn tells of heating valves in the locked attic being turned inexplicably on.

The ghost at the Inn By The Sea isn't always invisible, though. Guests have seen a woman in white pacing the beach at the back of the Inn, but she leaves no footprints in the sand. Pool-hopping teens had encountered the ghost several years ago. They'd snuck in during the night to swim and saw a woman in a light, glowing gown watching them. At the time, none of them had heard of Lydia Carver or the shipwreck of the schooner Charles. In another ghostly encounter, a guest of the Inn was walking along the beach on July 12, the anniversary of the wreck, when he heard sounds coming from the sea: timbers cracking and breaking followed by screams and shrieks. He was convinced he'd heard a shipwreck not far from the beach and the terrible cries of her passengers, but later learned that the sounds he'd heard were from a shipwreck that occurred one hundred eighty years ago.

Lydia's tall, slate-gray headstone reads: "Sacred to the memory of Miss Lydia Carver, daughter of Mr. Amos Carver of Freeport. Age 21. Who with 15 other passengers, male and female, perished in the merciless waves of the shipwreck of the schooner Charles. Captain Jacob Adams bound from Boston to Portland on a reef of rocks near the shore of Richmond's Island on Sunday night, July 12, 1807."

The wreck of the Charles inspired poet Thomas Shaw of Standish, Maine to write a 29-verse lament titled *Melancholy Shipwreck*. Sixteen black coffins surrounded the original print ballad. It is also the inspiration behind the Icarus Witch song 'The Ghost of Xavier Holmes' on their 2005 CD Capture the Magic.

Grave of Lydia Carver in Cape Elizabeth, a shipwrecked bride to be.
Courtesy of Bob Gray.

Pond Cove

Every summer, on a certain night, a spectral light mysteriously rises out of the water at Casco Bay and drifts to the shore at Pond Cove where it is said to cast a glare upon an old house by the beach before it vanishes. It is believed the light first appeared the night local fisherman Jack Welch disappeared.

Ten years afterward, a trio of fishermen was rowing into Pond Cove, hoping to reach shore before dark. The fog was creeping in and it was late as they reached the wharf and tied up their boat. Suddenly, the fog parted and from the clearing a pale flaming ball blasted toward them. Tom Wright saw it coming and dove to the deck of the boat, hands covering his head. The strange and frightful orb played along the rigging of their boat, and then flew shoreward to Tom Wright's house.

Pond Cove in Cape Elizabeth was the site of murder and supernatural revenge. *Courtesy Bob Gray.*

That very night, Tom Wright vanished.

Twenty years later, Wright's wife was distressed by the arrival of a letter from her husband. Written from his deathbed, in some distant place, it was a confession of murder. Tom Wright and Jack Welch had been romantic rivals, both wanting to court her. Tom knew she liked Jack better and was going to choose to marry him. In a fit of raging jealousy, Tom Wright murdered Jack Welch and disposed of his body at sea. He said in his letter that the spirit of Jack Welch had pursued him ever since and that his dying would finally put an end to it. However, that was not to be. Every year that mysterious light still rises from Casco Bay and drifts to shore to glare upon the house where Jack Welch might have lived with the woman he loved had he not been murdered so many years ago.

(14) Jewell Island, Casco Bay

In 1637, George Jewell of Barnstable, Massachusetts (or Saco, Maine, according to Folsom), was said to have bought the island from Indians, paying for it with gunpowder, rum and fishhooks. He later drowned in Boston Harbor. Stories about pirates on Jewell Island are typical of briny tales told up and down the coast: Captain William Kidd was said to have buried treasure in one of Jewell Island's caves, as did Captain Ann Bonney, who calmly shot some of her crew so their ghosts would guard her loot. Several stone markers were found in the 1960s that some believed were the graves of Bonney's victims. Pirate Captain Chase and his sidekick Kief are thought to have buried loot near Punch Bowl Cove. Among their many misdeeds, they lit lanterns and lured ships to nearby Cliff Island where they'd kill survivors and plunder the wreckage.

Historian Peter Benoit states that the treasure stories may have come from the island's name. Iron pyrite (fool's gold) mining on

Jewell may have eventually transformed linguistically from "pyrite" into "pirate" gold. Whatever the case may be, not all the Jewell Island ghosts have pirate connections. During World War II, the island was fortified and garrisoned by the military. According to eyewitnesses, the ghosts of some of those soldiers never left the island, even though no one lives there now.

Captain Elijah Jones had a farm on the island and made a modest living until he met George Vigny of St. Johns, Canada. Vigny had what he believed to be Captain Kidd's treasure map, and perhaps for this reason, Jones befriended him. Not long after, Jones became a wealthy man. Vigny, it was thought, took his share of the booty and went back to Canada.

About that time, islanders began seeing a strange and disturbing specter: the ghost of a man with blood running from his mouth and chest. They assumed it was one of those pirate spirits rumored to guard buried loot. Several years after Captain Jones died, his house became a virtual hotbed of poltergeist activity: screaming voices and flying chairs. Rum soaking the floor led to a hoard of hidden barrels and an elaborate tunnel system leading to hidden coves.

Not long after Jones' death, a farmer plowing near the southeastern shore found a human skeleton wedged between rocks at the wood's edge. A silver ring bearing the initials 'G.V.' indicated that the remains must be those of George Vigny. Now anyone could guess how Captain Jones got his money—he and Vigny had worked together to locate the pirate loot—and Jones must have killed Vigny and taken all the wealth. Assuming the bloody specter haunting the island was probably the ghost of George Vigny, an attempt was made to pacify the restless spirit with lamb's blood poured upon the place where his remains were found. It's not known if the blood worked its spell, but it would probably take more than lamb's blood to stop the strange lights, pirate ghosts and orbs moving along Jewell Island's deserted shores at night.

(15) Portland

Portland Art Museum
97 Spring Street

Captain Asa Clapp was born March 15, 1762 in Mansfield, Massachusetts and died April 17, 1848 at his home in Portland, Maine. Enlisting to fight in the American Revolution before the age of sixteen, by the time he reached twenty-one, Clapp had established himself as an officer on a privateer ship, and later became one of Maine's most wealthy and distinguished merchants. He married Elizabeth Wendell (Quincy), niece of Declaration of Independence signer, John Hancock. The hospitality of their mansion, Clapp House, was extended to military officers visiting Portland during and after the War of 1812. Dignified guests included U.S. Presidents James Monroe and James K. Polk. When Captain Clapp died, he was the oldest member of Portland's First Parish Church.

Mary Jane Clapp, granddaughter of Captain Clapp, was a well-known and well-loved philanthropist. She was also more than a bit eccentric. A recluse, she lived alone and kept her mansion like a museum until her death on September 9, 1920. Her will turned out to be one of the longest and most meticulous will and testaments in Cumberland County's history. She generously donated much of her estate to charities such as The Portland Widows' Wood Society, Maine General Hospital and the First Parish Church. (With certain stipulations that these institutions dedicate areas to the Clapp memory and adorn walls with their portraits.) As long as surviving family members remained married, they were also included in her will. Whoever divorced was disinherited.

Did Miss Clapp fear her own ghost being trapped in this world, unable to detach itself from her possessions? If so, as she requested, upon her death, the Clapp family coach, the four-poster bed upon which her father (Asa William Henry Clapp) died in 1799, and her Pierce Arrow car were given to no one but were to be burned instead. She also stated that upon its sale to commercial interests (businesses had been pressuring Mary Jane to sell), the Asa Clapp House would be torn down.

The seven-story Clapp Memorial Building built in 1924 stands on the lot where the Asa Clapp House once stood. The nearby Charles Q. Clapp House with its Greek columns belongs to the Maine College of Art and is listed on the National Register of Historic Places. Visitors, students and instructors at the Clapp House at 97 Spring Street have reported hearing the sounds of a woman sobbing and some have seen a translucent form of the crying woman wearing a long, old-fashioned dress.

Western Cemetery
Vaughn Street

The Western Cemetery is the second oldest graveyard in Portland with headstones dating from 1829 to 1987. According to Pete Wagner of Ghosts R Us, a Portland-based ghost hunters group, Portland is "one of the most haunted spots on the Maine coast." He would know; he's had experiences with the paranormal for more than half a century. Some of Portland's hot spots are Western Cemetery, the area behind Hadlock Field, Deering Oaks, Portland Museum of Art, and along the railroad tracks. Perhaps the hauntings are due to a period of brutal violence in history. According to the Portland Monthly this area was one of the places where Abenaki Natives attacked settlers in the late 1600s.

The cemetery property was once part of George Bramhall's farm. George was killed near Deering Oaks in an Indian attack.

Over the years more than a few visitors to Portland's Western Cemetery have been spooked, hairs bristling on the nape of the neck, by an eerie feeling of being watched. Pete Wagner says it's one of the places where he's detected activity.

Portland's Western Cemetery, one of Maine's most haunted graveyards.

(16) Windham

Anderson Cemetery
River Road

Visitors at Anderson Cemetery have reported returning to their parked cars—only to find they have moved several feet forward or backward. Some find their car doors wide open, but nothing is stolen and no one is hiding inside or near the car. On spring nights, people have heard Indian war cries followed by the sobs of weeping women. Time may have forgotten why, but history remembers.

On May 14, 1756, when Windham was called Presumscot and was part of New Marblehead, Massachusetts Bay Colony, Sokokis Chief Polin (some sources say Polan) and members of the Aucocisco Tribe (Abenaki and Pennacook tribes combined) attacked and massacred settlers on their way to tend their fields. This battle was known as Chief Polin's Last Raid.

The Natives' lives depended largely upon the river; they ate fish and used them to fertilize their crops. Beginning in 1732, the settlers constructed dams across the river. These dams ran sawmills and gristmills—and settlers often fought among themselves for rights to the river. Chief Polin went to Boston and appealed to the governor of the Bay Colony, who ordered fish ways for salmon, shad and alewives built on the river. Unfortunately, he was unable to enforce this.

The raid at Presumscot didn't last long; almost as soon as it started, Chief Polin was shot by musket and died on the spot. According to an eyewitness account, the air was filled "with yells of rage" as the Natives carried their dead chief to their canoes. They paddled up the river to Sebago Lake and buried Chief Polin beneath the roots of a beech tree because they feared what the settlers might do to his body.

A wooden marker on Anderson Road reads: "Site of Chief Polin's Death, May 14, 1756."

During the raid, settler Ephraim Winship was said to have been scalped not once but twice, yet he survived for a decade after the ordeal. According to Windham historian, Samuel Thomas Dole, the death of Chief Polin ended the settlers' troubles with the Natives in the area.

Peace may have existed with the ones who survived that last raid ... but what of those who didn't? On both sides, ghosts may be reliving their deaths; hence the eerie sounds of war cries and weeping that haunt Anderson Road. In September 1998, a group of friends saw a "translucent face with glowing eyes" in the window of a house on the River Road.

The moving of parked cars, however, is another mystery yet to be solved.

Brown Cemetery
9 Chute Road

Sometimes at dawn, two little girls are seen playing in Brown Cemetery in Windham. The cemetery is old, surrounded by a wooden fence in a heavily wooded area. Some of the graves date back to the late 1700s. The grounds are well kept, however there are several unmarked and sunken graves. And, some of the headstones are broken.

The little girls aren't always dressed for the weather; they wear old-fashioned clothes: long ankle-length dresses with wool stockings and sunbonnets. Giggling, they chase one another in a game of tag, hiding behind headstones and popping back out again, racing back and forth along the roadside at the front of the cemetery. Seeing them play, a person would think they're very much alive. They're not.

They are the ghosts of two sisters whose grave markers are here, however their graves are empty. It is believed that the girls died when they fell into an old well or a mineshaft. Their bodies were never recovered.

(17) Naples Historical Society Museum
Village Green, Naples

Thirty miles northwest of Portland, on Route 302, in a building just behind the Methodist Church, the Naples Historical Society Museum houses a haunted object said to be cursed—a golden idol stolen from a Buddhist temple in the Tientsin Province during the Chinese Boxer Rebellion (1898-1900). Merchants in the tea trade, brothers Charles and Ruben Hill brought it from China to Naples, Maine. Charles was a sea captain who lived for several years in China and helped build China's first railroad. According to stories told about them, they looted the temple, holding the monks at bay under threat of gunfire, and took as many as four golden statues. The monk leader said something to the brothers that brought terror to the faces of his fellow monks, but neither Charles nor Ruben understood his words. The statues weren't solid gold, as they had first believed, but were gold leaf plated wood. One was hollow inside, but not entirely empty—it contained a clutch of rare jewels. The Hill brothers sold the jewels for $300,000 and built "Belvue Terrace," a sixteen-room, three-story mansion. Here in the grand main hall of their stately home, they displayed the largest of the statues, a seven-foot temple guard.

But their fortune was short-lived. Both brothers died mysteriously, leading their neighbors and relatives to believe the idols had something to do with their deaths. No one is sure how they died, but most agree that Charles died first. One version of their deaths has them returning to the temple in Tientsin for more booty and were executed by order of the temple priest. Others believe Charles contracted a fever in China and died in a Yokohama, Japan hospital. Ruben died a short time later in an automobile accident. Heirs of the estate gave the guardian statue to the Boston Museum of Fine Arts, while the smaller statues were either tossed into Long Lake or buried on or near the brothers' property.

This didn't stop the bad luck ... for almost every owner of the Hill estate thereafter was plagued by disease, sadness, madness and death. For instance, Charles White, son of the estate's second owner, was murdered on the Portland waterfront. The third owner, Charles Soden, and his wife opened Belvue Terrace as "the Hayloft," a restaurant-antique shop. Then Charles hung himself and Belvue Terrace was bought by Philip and Dorothy Clark, who renamed it 'Serenity Hill.' In February 1951, a fire destroyed Serenity Hill. Philip Clark's body was found in the basement. Dorothy was institutionalized and died in a mental hospital. A church group then bought it and their pastor moved his mobile home onto the old foundation of the mansion, but then the pastor and his wife divorced and moved away. It was then sold to another church group who held services in the carriage house at Serenity Hill, but their pastor stole church funds and ran off. The most recent tragedy was in 2001 when the owner's son developed and died from leukemia.

A Chinese guardsman rests in this Naples museum.

Eventually, the largest statue was recovered from the Boston Museum of Fine Arts and given to the Naples Historical Society Museum where it was put on display. It remains there to this day. Apparently no one dares take the risk of stealing it a second time. The museum is located at Naples Village Green on Route 302 next to Grange Hall and the Edward I. Singer Community Center (in front of the post office). It is open from July through August from 10 a.m. to 2 p.m.

(18) Route 26, New Gloucester

According to local lore, Route 26 near the Shaker Village was the site of a grisly car accident that killed a New Gloucester couple. The woman's ghost has been seen by many people wandering along the road, and some report seeing the ghost of a man following her.

According to the Maine Department of Transportation, no less than nine deadly car accidents have occurred on Route 26 since 1963. The most dangerous places for accidents on Route 26 are between Range Hill Road at Shaker Hill and Birchwood Lane as well as between Snow Hill and Pond roads (known locally as "Seven Deadly Curves"). The Shaker Village, established in 1794 as the Sabbathday Lake Shaker Community, is the last remaining Shaker village with practicing members.

Route 26, New Gloucester

(19) The Desert of Maine
95 Desert Road, Freeport
www.desertofmaine.com

When you think of Maine, you probably picture pine trees and seascapes. A desert is probably the last thing you'd associate with Vacationland, but there is indeed a desert in Freeport, Maine. This desert is actually a deposit of glacial silt (not sand). The silt was exposed by topsoil erosion caused by a farm's failure to rotate crops and the overgrazing of animals. The glacier that carried the silt deposit is the same one that carved Maine's unique typography at the end of the last Ice Age, about eleven thousand years ago.

It is a unique place; there are only three other 'deserts' like it in the world (Alaska, Washington and Denmark). At the Desert of Maine, the tops of giant pines poke out of dunes more than fifty feet deep. The silt glitters like gold in the sun because of the amount of mica it contains.

The desert, now slightly more than forty acres, was once a lush three hundred-acre farm that belonged to the William Tuttle family in 1797. After erosion exposed the underlying silt, it gradually grew from the size of a dinner plate to a point where the desert overcame their farm. The Tuttles sold the land in 1919 for $300 to Henry Goldrup. He conducted desert tours at ten cents each. He brought in a camel named Sadie to offer camel rides, and it was during this period that he discovered a freshwater spring. This resulted in a swimming pool, concession stands and campgrounds—and locals dubbing it a "tourist trap." Back then, skeptics speculated that the owner had sand hauled in by the truckloads.

There is another story of how the desert came to be. According to legend, the original landowner had several sons, but his youngest was the one most interested in farming. After the farmer's wife died, the farmer married a widow with a son of her own. On his deathbed, he made his second wife promise to leave the farm to his youngest biological son, who wanted to continue the family farm. The second wife went against her husband's dying wish and gave the farm to her own son … and while he was farming it, the desert formed. Those who believe the legend also say that somewhere near the old springhouse, well buried under sand, is a stone sculpture of a giant head with long pointed ears and a wide laughing mouth.

The desert is open from early May to mid-October. There are admission fees; visit www.desertofmaine.com for updates.

(20) River Road, Brunswick

Five mysterious stone markers can be found along River Road in Brunswick, where it is said that during a full moon, voices and singing can be heard. Are these the sounds of Native American ghosts? Throughout the years, many people have studied the stones, but no one knows their purpose or significance.

(21) Harpswell

The town of Harpswell is rich with history, legends, and fishing tradition. A unique bridge connects Bailey and Orrs islands; it was constructed in 1928 of granite blocks laid in crib fashion (lengthwise over crosswise) without cement or mortar of any kind. The Meeting House built in 1759 in Harpswell Center may be the oldest meetinghouse still standing in Maine.

Nearby Pond Island has a reputation for being haunted by the ghost of a local rogue named John Darling. John lived on Pond Island in exile from the mainland for over twenty years, according to writer Neil Rolde in *So You Think You Know Maine*. Rumor has it Darling froze to death there and his ghost still haunts the island.

While not a ghost story, this was an interesting tidbit: according to *Haunted New England* by Mary Bolte, Harpswell's Pond Island was home to a self-proclaimed alchemist in 1801 known only as "The Professor". He told several people that he knew how to turn morning dew into pure silver. Dew was promptly collected and taken out to Pond Island where it was poured into the Professor's kettle over an outdoor fire. Needless to say, silver didn't materialize. For his next trick, the Professor claimed that the dew hadn't been handled properly, so he repeated the process, sneaking in a bit of previously molten silver droplets into the pot. Discovering silver in the pot, the locals were now convinced enough to pay "The Professor" to make more silver. His third trick worked like magic: indeed he made silver from dew—by pocketing the cash and leaving town lickety-split.

According to some, Pond Island is home to a ghost that guards a keg of gold. A pirate who went by the surname Lowe supposedly buried gold somewhere in the dried-up pond on the small island. Prospective gold diggers who've remained after dark claim they've seen a ghostly man walking around their digging area. Some believe it's the ghost of the pirate Lowe.

A ghost horse has been heard on Bailey Island. People living there have heard the unmistakable sounds of galloping hooves approaching, but the horse is never seen.

Hannah Stover, 'the witch of Harpswell', lived at the southern tip of Harpswell Neck in the 1700s. She wasn't really a witch by any means—she was a Quaker from Freeport, Maine, the second wife of Elkanah Stover (the Stovers were a family of shipbuilders in South Harpswell). Some people thought her a witch because she didn't attend church at the Meeting House. When she died, her neighbors refused to carry her coffin to the Meeting House for a Christian burial. They wanted her buried in the Indian graveyard out by Cundy's Harbor. Shortly thereafter, many who didn't want Hannah buried in "sacred ground" began hearing strange noises inside their homes, disembodied footsteps walking across their floors at night, and several instances of poltergeist-like activity. Within a week, the good women of Harpswell took it upon themselves to carry the coffin of Goodwife Stover to Harpswell Center. At the Meeting House, Ezra Johnson accused Hannah of being a "witch wife", saying his cow had been bewitched and his fishing seine had been mysteriously broken. He also said he had heard Hannah's voice in the wind as he encountered rough seas on his way to Potts Point. Hannah's stepdaughter, Mercy Stover, and Goody Cole reminded everyone of Hannah's gentle spirit and how much she'd helped her neighbors. The women then carried her coffin to the Meeting House graveyard and buried Hannah themselves. After she was properly interred in the town cemetery all the strange activity and noises ceased.

Harpswell's most famous ghost is the dreaded ghost ship that forecasted an omen of death to members of the village. As told in the 1866 poem by John Greenleaf Whittier, the ghost ship was sighted just before the death of a Harpswell resident, usually someone related to one of the crew aboard the ill-fated Dash. The Dash was the subject of another poem by Elisa Dennison Long, which was published in *Three Centuries of Freeport, Maine* by Florence G. Thurston (Anthoensen Press, Portland, Maine 1940).

The Dash was a schooner built at Porter's Landing in Freeport in the early 1800s for William Porter of Portland and Samuel Porter of Freeport. She was commissioned by the U.S. Government in June 1812 as a privateer ship, a sort of legalized piracy that allowed the confiscation of enemy ships, cargo and crew in times of war. During the War of 1812, the United States commissioned over one hundred fifty private ships as privateers since they only had fourteen Naval warships.

The Dash proved herself a formidable warship in at least fifteen successful voyages in three years; during this time it also transported rum, molasses and coffee from ports in distant Bermuda and Haiti. In January 1815, the Dash, piloted by her third captain, and her sister ship, the Champlain (some sources say the Chamberlain) set sail from Portland and after two days encountered a storm at sea. The Champlain turned away from the storm—the Dash didn't and became lost in gale winds and frigid seas. The captain's wife, Lois, had a premonition the night the Dash disappeared; she knew she'd never see her husband alive again. Not so for the Dash, which has been spotted sailing out of the fog in full mast on a dead wind in Casco Bay, mainly sighted around Bailey's and Orr's islands.

As a ghost ship, the Dash was seen twice by Captain James Dawn. First, just before the death of his first wife and son and a second time, just before his own death. Captain Toothaker saw the ghost ship before jumping overboard to his death; Polly Toothaker saw it in the 1880s during the daytime at the exact moment of her husband's death. All who died were related in some way to crewmen aboard the Dash.

In August 1942, while the Navy and Coast Guard were patrolling Casco Bay, Homer Grimm and a lady friend had rowed out to Punkin Nubb for a little privacy. They had no idea that something moving had shown up as a blip on the radar on the nearby military ships and were startled by the sudden blare of sirens. Just then, an old-fashioned, tall-masted ship with fog-laden wind in her sails and the name Dash—Freeport on the stern glided past them and disappeared into the mist. At the same time, she also vanished from the radar screens. Homer couldn't believe his eyes—the Dash was the same privateer ship that disappeared one hundred thirty years before!

If you see the Dash, it will probably be around dusk, always in the fog, sailing under full sail and straight ahead. Sometimes its course is toward Freeport, other times it sweeps toward the docks of the islands, and then it simply disappears or suddenly stops and retreats back into the fog. Throughout the years, the ghost ship has been spotted at Lookout Point in Harpswell Center, Potts Point in South Harpswell, and at Bailey and Orrs' islands. But keep in mind that unless you're willing to join her crewmen, it isn't advisable to look for the ghost ship if your ancestors were crewmen aboard the Dash.

Another ghost ship seen at Harpswell Harbor is the schooner Sarah, built at the Soule Boatyard in South Freeport for two young friends: George Leverett and Charles Jose, both of Portland, Maine. While their ship was under construction, they met Sarah Soule and, although both men fell madly in love with her, she chose George as her beau. The friendship between George and Charles ended when Charles attempted to throw George in the Royal River. Soon there-after, Charles disappeared and George, now sole owner, named his ship Sarah after his lovely fiancé. After their marriage, he managed to round up a crew and they sailed the Sarah to Portland to fill the hold with cargo bound for the West Indies. The Don Pedro Sala-zar, a strange black ship, followed the Sarah out of Portland on her southern voyage. The Sarah's crew, nervous about being followed, successfully petitioned George to report the Don Pedro Salazar to the British Admiralty in Nassau, but before they could reach harbor, the Don Pedro Salazar opened fire upon the Sarah, killing everyone but Captain George Leverett. Imagine George's surprise when the Don Pedro Salazar's captain boarded the Sarah and George found himself face to face with his former friend and rival, Charles Jose. After looting the Sarah, Charles bound George to the mainmast and turned the ship's wheel seaward, leaving George to die. In his eventual delirium, George thought he saw his dead crewmen rising upright to set the sails and change course for home.

That November in Pott's Point, several people saw the Sarah sail into harbor where it stopped to lower a man into a rowboat, silently bringing him safely to shore. Captain George Leverett was found lying unconscious on a rock with his logbook beside him. The rower returned to the Sarah, which disappeared in the fog.

The last report of anyone sighting the Sarah was on a 1880s summer afternoon by a guest at the Harpswell House, but of course that's not to say she's gone for good.

(22) Poland

Route 26

On the night of October 6, 1856, Mary Knight was viciously attacked while sleeping, her throat slashed in the dark. The coroner stated that she probably died within seconds, but in truth, she had suffered for a long time before her death.

Mary was married to Solomon Knight, but after he died in 1840, his brother George expressed interest in her and won her hand in 1843. Their marriage was a bit of a scandal (although it was perfectly Biblical for a man to marry his brother's widow). The problem was their ages; Mary was 47, George was 23. Eventually, gossip about them died down or people found another target to talk about. George took over Solomon's farm and Mary, a mother of seven children from her first marriage, kept the homestead. Lydia Knight, George and Solomon's mother, lived with them, as did thirteen-year-old Hannah S. Partridge and ten-year-old Sidney Verrill. Hannah was a distant relative; Sidney was a farm apprentice who planned to live with the Knights until adulthood.

Lydia, Hannah and Sidney were inside the house at the time of the murder. Sidney was first to awaken. He heard Mary call out for Hannah and then plead with someone else. She screamed several times. Hannah woke up, lit a candle and shook Lydia awake, and then all three went to the room where Mary had been sleeping. Hannah saw the fleeting shadow of a person cross the room, but she couldn't identify who it was. They found Mary lying dead in a blood-soaked bed. Stricken, Sidney ran to a neighbor's home for help.

The man of the house, George Knight, wasn't home for most of the night. Around 7 p.m., Mary's husband of thirteen years had taken a team of oxen to neighbor Israel Herrick's barn where he loaded shingles onto his wagon. He told Herrick he was going to the nearby town of Gray. He hadn't gone far when he stopped his team on a seldom-used road and hurried back home under the cover of darkness.

Just a few months earlier, in August, Mary had written a daughter that she feared George was trying to poison her. Indeed something was wrong—she couldn't seem to keep food down and she'd taken ill with bouts of vomiting. She was seen by doctors and her condition confounded all of them. Of course, she couldn't reveal her suspicions, not with George standing nearby. She grew sicker and weaker ... but her death didn't come fast enough for George, who complained that Mary was old and "used up," unable to bear him sons of his own. It was believed he had taken a lover.

Although he never confessed, there was enough evidence against him to merit an arrest three days after Mary's murder. His trial lasted twenty days and was attended by hundreds of people with enough interest to garner a mention in The New York Times. After twenty-five hours of deliberation, a jury found George Knight guilty of first-degree murder and sentenced him to death. Governor Joshua Chamberlain commuted George Knight's death sentence to life imprisonment. Twenty years later, Maine became the fifth state to abolish the death penalty.

The earliest sighting of Mary Knight's ghost was in August 1929 when Mr. and Mrs. Donald Tully were on their way home to South Paris. They had been visiting Donald's brother in Portland. On Route 26, late at night, they stopped to offer a ride to a woman standing by the road in a billowy white dress. She accepted the ride and gave the couple some startling advice: Donald's brother was soon to die—and if Donald wanted to keep his hardware store, he'd best pull out of the stock market as soon as possible. She told them she needed to go to the old George Knight murder site.

Another sighting occurred on May 15, 1945 at 4:15 a.m. Judge Roy Sloan was headed west on Route 26, on his way to a murder trial in Bethel. After cresting a hill, he saw a lady wearing a white dress standing in the middle of the road. He stopped and she told him she needed a ride. After she got into his car, she told him that James Beacon murdered his brother-in-law with a knife that he'd hidden beneath the back steps of his mother's house. This news shocked the judge; the murder weapon had yet to be found, and her knowledge of the crime raised his suspicions. She then informed him he would remarry in exactly two years and two weeks from this day.

At 10:30 p.m., on July 7, 1957, Alice Foster was driving to the Poland Spring Inn. Her parents were there and she had a week's vacation. Seeing a woman in white standing in the road ahead, she stopped to ask the stranger if she needed a lift. The woman accepted the ride, and told Alice that she'd been waiting for her to come along. She then said that Alice would soon be starting a residency at a hospital. This was true, although there was no way the stranger could have known it. She then went on to say that in the near future, Alice would be blamed for a patient's death. Alice would be asked to resign, which she must not do, for ultimately, it would be proven that a supervisor was the one responsible. Alice would go on to be a wonderful doctor. Before Alice had a chance to react to this strange prophesy, the lady added that she was going to the Knight murder site.

On a June night in 1967, Jeffrey Blessins was driving toward Portland via Route 26 when he had to swerve to avoid hitting a pedestrian, a woman in a white dress standing in the middle of the road. He stopped the car, backed up and asked if she was okay and if she needed a ride. She accepted and told him she had important news for him.

As he drove, she told Jeffrey that he'd soon be leaving for Vietnam. It was true; he had orders to leave that Sunday. She said he'd be in an air crash—but that he'd come out of it alive. She then added that he should never give up hope, that a bright future was in store for him. The last thing she said was that she was headed for the George Knight murder site just up the road.

Amazingly, the lady in white gave these folks some very accurate prophesies. Donald Tully's brother died and because of her advice, the Tullys avoided the stock market crash that became an impetus for the Great Depression. Judge Sloan ordered an investigation of Mrs. Beacon's property—and the bloodstained knife was discovered under her back steps. Sloan remarried exactly two years and two weeks after giving the lady in white a ride.

As a resident intern in a Massachusetts hospital, Alice Foster was accused of causing a patient's death and was asked to resign. She refused and was later cleared of every allegation against her. She continues to practice medicine in the Boston area.

On his third day in Vietnam, Jeffrey Blessins survived a helicopter crash and was then captured and held as a P.O.W. for four long months. He managed to escape and later, went to college. After earning a degree, he became a clinical psychologist, a pioneer in studies of Post Traumatic Stress Disorder and the delayed stress response.

These are just a sample of the stories about Mary Knight, the lady in white of Route 26. She was sixty-one when she lost her life, but she often appears as a young woman. She wears the white flowing nightgown she died in. However, it makes one wonder why she haunts this road in particular.

We may never know, but if you are lucky enough to see her, you'll be wise to stop and offer her a ride. She always has a prophetic message for her thoughtful drivers. You won't need to stop to let her out for she'll vanish in an instant.

The Poland Spring Resort
41 Ricker Road
www.polandspringps.org

Before Europeans colonized America, the Poland Spring was used by the Native Americans who lived here. For a people who recognized the divinity of the Great Spirit in all things, living and non-living, the spring with its cool, sweet water made this a sacred area. The famous Abenaki healer, Mollyockett, revered these springs for their healing qualities. Eventually, Shakers moved to the area and used the land as pastures for their cattle. In 1793, Jabez Ricker bought the 200-acre Poland Spring land and one small log cabin from the Shakers by trading a mill and land he owned in Alfred, Maine. Jabez, his wife Mary, and their ten children moved to Poland Spring.

The main road divided their property, making it the perfect rest spot for travelers on their way to Montreal from Boston. With his sons Wentworth, Samuel and Joseph, Jabez built a gable-roofed inn and hung a sign over the door that read: Wentworth Ricker 1797. As business thrived, it became the "best known Inn in northern Massachusetts." Ricker's descendants would go on to create the publishing company, Hiram Ricker & Sons, and their descendants would build the golf course at Poland Spring in August 1896, the first of its kind in America owned by a resort.

Jabez Ricker died seven years after Maine became a state. Wentworth Ricker developed what doctors determined an incurable kidney disease. He found his cure in the Poland Spring water and returned to robust health. He then constructed Route 26, the road connecting Portland, Maine with Paris, Maine. Healthful Poland Spring water, enjoyed by members of the Ricker family as well as their many guests, went commercial in 1845 when doctors – hearing of Poland Spring water's healing qualities – began ordering the water for their patients. Soon thereafter, almost every traveler in America had access to Poland Spring water.

In 1876, descendant Hiram Ricker built a grand, one hundred-room hotel. These rooms were so popular that reservations for them were often placed years in advance. The Poland Spring Inn expanded to three hundred rooms and its most famous guests included celebrities like Babe Ruth, Betty Grable, Judy Garland, Charles Lindbergh, John D. Rockefeller, Alexander Graham Bell, and Presidents Coolidge, Taft, and Harding, as well as many of the Kennedy family, and the Maharishi Yogi.

In 1893, the Rickers bought the Maine State Building displayed at the 1891 Columbia Exposition in Chicago. Sixteen freight cars shipped it to Poland Spring, Maine. In 1906/1907, a new springhouse and bottling plant was built. The All Souls Chapel opened in 1912 and Poland Spring's Presidential Inn opened in 1913. It was to be the last hotel the Rickers built. In 1962, Saul Feldman of Boston purchased the Poland Spring Resort, its buildings and land. He added the Maine Inn to the Poland Spring complex.

The Poland Spring Resort is haunted by Hiram Ricker, founder of the Poland Spring Water® Company. Several employees have reported seeing his ghost walking about, especially at the Presidential Inn. Some workers have heard his voice coming from vacant rooms. The sounds of his footsteps have been heard in the early hours of the morning in the empty lobby, and his sense of humor lives on as he occasionally moves objects to unusual places.

The ghost of a woman was seen in 2006 behind the Maine Inn, and the entertainer who saw her there refuses to leave the building alone at night.

Visitors are welcome in the Water Museum, the All Souls Chapel, and the Maine State Building, which is a museum of Ricker family memorabilia. It is listed on the National Register of Historic Places and is open everyday (except Mondays) from Memorial Day to Columbus Day with a $4 admission.

The Presidential Inn at the Poland Springs Resort.

(23) Schaeffer Theater
305 College Street,
Bates College, Lewiston

Bates Theater was built in 1960 and renamed as Schaeffer Theater in 1972 for Professor Lavinia Miriam Schaeffer. It seats an audience of over two hundred souls and is occasionally visited by the ghost of Professor Schaeffer. She was director of Dramatics at Bates College from 1938 to 1968 and the chairman of the Speech Department from 1969 to 1972. She died in 1978.

To her students, this beloved teacher was "a sparkle of spirit, moving and speaking in accents and rhythms that were undeniably different and exciting." But when things go wrong onstage at the Schaeffer Theater, the lights sometimes flicker or doors may suddenly swing open or shut on their own. It is said that if you can detect a sudden whiff of Chanel No. 5 in the air, you can be certain Professor Schaeffer is present, still keeping her eye on the stage and its actors.

Sagadahoc County

North Cemetery, Montsweag Roadhouse, Sequin Island Lighthouse

(24) North Cemetery, Bowdoin

Called 'Cemetery in the Pit,' the North Cemetery is located diagonally across the road from where the old Bunker Chase Tavern used to be, on the corner of Dead River and Litchfield roads. In its heyday, the tavern was an inn belonging to the Litchfield-Bowdoin Stage Line that ran from Brunswick to Augusta. The Old North Church, thought to be the oldest meetinghouse in Bowdoin, sat adjacent to the cemetery. In recent years, members of the Bowdoin Historical Society have been restoring North Cemetery.

According to legend, a local woman named Elizabeth was accused by her neighbors of practicing witchcraft. No documentation exists of any condemned witch executions taking place on the Maine frontier during the Colonial Era, however such stories (i.e., Belfast's Barbara Houndsworth and the "leg" witch of Bucksport) persist to this day. In what is now Bowdoin, Maine, Elizabeth, they say, was hung by a lynch mob and was buried in an unmarked grave next to a large tree stump in what would later become North Cemetery. A bright orb of light resembling a star has been seen to appear here on certain nights, and although her grave remains unmarked by stones, a circle of trees surrounds it. Legend has it that her grave itself is cursed—and if anyone dares step into that circle of trees, the curse is on them. They say that's what happened to three boys who tried desecrating Lizzie's grave—every one of them died in accidents the very same week. Various ghost hunter websites have short write-ups about Lizzie's grave and all of them end with a word of caution.

(25) Montsweag Roadhouse
Route 1, Woolwich

Since January 2006, Chris and Jenny Johnson have owned Montsweag Roadhouse. From the 1950s, when the Sewell family converted their barn at Montsweag Farm into the Montsweag Restaurant, the establishment has seen several changes and a succession of owners over the years. The original structure was built as an apple barn, a place to sort and distribute apples. After farm workers sorted the apples, the fruits were lowered to the first story through doors in the ceiling, then packed into waiting carts that took them to markets along the East Coast.

In October 2002, Paul and Liz Cooleen purchased the Montsweag Restaurant and renamed it Cooleen's Restaurant. They couldn't help but notice the unusual bright spots that kept showing up in photographs taken there. In an interview published in Plymouth Magazine, Paul told reporter Terry Rayno about a five or six-year-old boy who asked about a stranger in the restaurant that, apparently, no one else could see. By the boy's description, Paul suspected it might be the ghost of a former chef who worked there years ago.

Dine with a ghost at Montsweag Roadhouse in Woolwich.

(26) Sequin Island Lighthouse, Georgetown

Sequin Island isn't named for or even pronounced like the decorations on a lady's dress; instead the word 'Sequin' is as close as English settlers could come to pronouncing the Abenaki word meaning "place where the sea vomits," a fitting description for just about any rockbound island in the guts of the Atlantic. It is properly pronounced SEE-gwin. Island lighthouses, often separated from the mainland by miles of ocean, are desolate, lonely places to live, and sometimes the isolation of living in one proves too much to bear, as illustrated by the following story, and it's interesting to note that the next lighthouse keeper's journal made mention of piano music playing in the night.

First commissioned in 1795 by President George Washington, Sequin Island Light is the second oldest lighthouse (Portland Head Light has the honor of being the first) in North America. It is located 2.5 miles from Popham Beach and stands one hundred eighty feet above mean water.

In the 1850s, a new lighthouse keeper and his bride, their names long forgotten, moved out to Sequin Island. They were the only people there and it wasn't long before the new wife began feeling depressed, evidently missing her friends and family on the mainland. To please her, the lighthouse keeper bought her a piano. She could play a little bit, but only by reading the notes off sheet music. He must have thought the piano would keep her busy and might help stave off the loneliness she felt. As he carried the piano bench in from the boat, it must have tipped, spilling the sheet music inside to the wind. He managed to salvage only one sheet. Some say her piano came with only one sheet of music, but pianos of that era often came with several sheets of popular music.

Regardless of how the single sheet of music came to be, the bride played it, no doubt delighting in the sounds that drowned out the wind and filled her new home with melody. She played that one song so often that she must have learned it by heart. Moreover, she played it repeatedly from morning to night. Her husband probably begged her to play something different, but she couldn't—she didn't have the sheet music for anything else. If he asked her to stop playing, she probably did at first, but then went right back to it as the music had become like a mantra to her.

Finally, the lighthouse keeper had enough of the constant song, which was firmly lodged in his brain. While she was playing, he took an axe to the instrument, smashing it to bits, and when she protested, he put the axe to her as well. Soaked in blood, with splinters of fine wood hanging from his sleeves, he killed himself … and did that stop the music?

No, say locals who live near Popham Beach, for on windless nights, unnatural piano music drifts from Sequin Island to the mainland. It would seem the lighthouse keeper and his piano-playing bride are stuck in the sequence of death replay. They are ghosts gone insane, but they are not alone.

A ghost known as 'Old Captain' resides at Sequin Island. He's a kindly, mischievous sort of spirit, sometimes lifting a tool or item, and then returning it back to the same place, to the bafflement of the living. He sweeps coats and caps off hooks and tosses them to the floor. His footsteps have been heard on the lighthouse stairs. Uncanny cold spots have been felt, mostly upstairs near the lens. Accompanying him is the spirit of a little girl. Her ghost has materialized running up and down the stairs; she sometimes waves at people and bounces a ball against a bedroom door. Her laughter has been heard, for she's a cheery soul—or she may be giggling at the antics of Old Captain. They sometimes are found together near the foghorn. The ghost of a woman has been seen outside the lighthouse as well as the silhouette of an unknown man in a window working inside.

According to the caretakers' log by Jack and Tobi Graham (on the Friends of Sequin Island website) on the morning of July 14, 2005, an oval platter Tobi had set by the stove while she was preparing breakfast suddenly exploded with a loud "POW". (She hadn't turned on the stove yet nor had she set anything on the platter.) It did not fall and crash to the floor—and no one had touched it. It literally exploded. Tiny shards of the platter were found everywhere. Shortly after that, while drying dishes, Jack noticed a broken mug that had been fine when he washed it moments before. The Grahams chalked both incidents up to the workings of a ghost.

Other keepers have witnessed doors swinging open and closing by themselves. Some have heard coughing when no one else was present.

The Seguin Island Light is a lovely historic relic with a long history that is accessible to private boaters. So many strange things have happened here that it is well worth a look for ghost hunters. The lighthouse is open to the public Memorial Day through Labor Day, and is accessible by boat from Bath, Popham Beach, or Boothbay Harbor. For information on tours, contact Friends of Seguin Island, Inc., P.O. Box 866, Bath, Maine 04530 or call 207-443-4808.

Lincoln County

(27) Wiscasset

Canfield's Restaurant
Main Street

In 1790, Charles and Lydia Dana built a boarding house that later became the East Wind Restaurant then the Wizard of Odds and Ends Antique Shop, and then Canfield's Restaurant, an eatery established by former owners Richard and Mary Ann Canfield. Located on Route 1, just past Pottle Cove Road, the restaurant is said to be haunted by a poltergeist-like ghost that many think may be the spirit of original owner Lydia Dana. It's her habit to upset tea cups, slap folks on their rumps, move chairs and unlatch doors, but she has never caused anyone harm and is affectionately addressed as 'Mother Dana' by those who are used to her antics.

The Marine Antique Shop
14 High Street

When this building was a restaurant, customers and staff sometimes experienced poltergeist activity—moving chairs, tables and dinnerware. Since it became an antique shop, things have quieted down a bit.

(28) Newcastle

Glidden Cemetery
River Road

Genealogical records show Colonel Joel Howe, Jr. was born November 2, 1748 in Worcester, Massachusetts. He was an officer in the Massachusetts Militia. He married Mary 'Molly' Gates on October 18, 1770 and after the War of 1812, he moved his family to a plot of land on what is now Elm and Hodgdon streets in Damariscotta, Maine.

Like most families of that era, the Howe family was large, comprised of five daughters and four sons: Daniel, Edwin, Emily, Joel III, Lorenzo, Sally, Mary, Janette and Josephene. A relative, Elias Howe, invented the sewing machine.

After the Colonel died, the Howes moved across the road and built Howe's Tavern, an inn run by Joel Howe, III, and it was the place to stop and rest in Damariscotta when traveling by stagecoach. The hotel register shows President James K. Polk among the notables who stayed there. Eventually, Howe's Tavern became The Plummer House, then the Joseph Melville King Memorial Hospital and later Clark's Apartments.

In 1882, Dr. Robert Dixon was called to the Howe residence by the town constable, who told him that the Howes' were keeping the corpse of their sister, Mary, inside the house. The family assured the constable that Mary was not dead, that she'd soon awaken, even though she hadn't moved in two weeks. As a physician and coroner, it was Dixon's job to examine her body and pronounce her dead or alive. The good doctor knew Mary Howe; he'd treated her broken ankle after she'd fallen while trying to fly from the top of a staircase.

The Howes were known for an avid interest in spiritualism, especially Edwin, Lorenzo and Mary, who excelled at contacting the dead, slipping into trances and speaking with ghosts, a feat that attracted people from all over New England. She accurately predicted the death of a relative of one of her guests, who was away in New York City. The lady asked Mary when he'd return to Damariscotta, and while in her trance, Mary told her, "When the lights appear, he will die."

When the gaslights of the Brooklyn Bridge were turned on for the very first time in its history, this certain man collapsed, dead from an apparent heart attack.

After that, the duration of Mary's trances began to lengthen. When Dr. Dixon arrived, he found Mary lying on a couch in the parlor surrounded by stones that had been placed around her body to keep her warm, even though it was summer. In his professional opinion, she looked asleep. Her supple flesh retained a healthy glow. She showed no stiffness or rigor mortis. She even smelled alive. Yet, upon closer examination, Mary didn't appear to be breathing and the doctor could find no traces of a heartbeat or pulse. Without breath and a beating heart, Dr. Dixon had no other choice than to pronounce Mary Howe dead. Despite her family's protests, her body was taken for immediate interment by the constable, a minister, and the undertaker's assistant. The town was outraged about this—many of them had been inside the Howe residence—they'd seen Mary in her trance and knew without a doubt that she was alive. Her brother Edwin insisted she would come out of her trance at any moment.

Benjamin Metcalf wouldn't allow Mary's burial at Hillside Cemetery. He knew Mary and couldn't believe she was dead. She'd been in trances before, sometimes as long as a week.

Mary was then transported to Glidden Cemetery in neighboring Newcastle, but believing they would be having a hand in causing her death, gravediggers refused to dig her grave. The constable, reverend and undertaker's assistant dug the grave themselves, but at the last moment, the undertaker's assistant couldn't bear to help lower her into the grave. She looked so alive, and the man likely had to turn away as the constable and minister buried her.

Now everyone, especially those who knew about her long trances, prayed in horror that Mary was actually dead, for death would be a blessing compared to waking up in a coffin with no way out. Her unmarked grave was meant to prevent anyone, however well intending, from digging her up.

After her burial, many people refused to visit or even walk past Glidden Cemetery, for the sounds of muffled moans and screams have been heard coming up from the burial ground. The strange behaviors of dogs being walked past the cemetery by their owners have been noticed as well. They'd stop suddenly and howl with their muzzles pointed at the sky. People have reported seeing strange mists and glowing lights drifting along the cemetery paths and between headstones. One November, Judson D. Hale, Sr., editor of *Yankee Magazine* and *The Old Farmer's Almanac*, visited Glidden Cemetery and in his book, *Inside New England*, he describes what he heard there as a "soft, short moan." Throughout the years, many have heard similar sounds. The only explanation for the mysterious lights, mists and noises is that they exist because Mary Howe was buried alive.

Jones Corner
Routes 213 and 215
Damariscotta Mills

Exactly what or who haunts Jones' Corner at the intersection of Routes 213 and 215 in Newcastle's Damariscotta Mills is anyone's guess. The property originally belonged to the descendants of Cornelius Jones, a mill man who moved to Newcastle in 1729; it stayed in the Jones family until 1921.

The *Damariscotta Herald* in 1896 described reports of "an evil eye glowering upon the territory known as Jones Woods" and how Samuel Michael Powers disappeared there, "unaccountably swallowed up", as well as another traveler who had left his horse unattended in Jones' pasture and was never seen again. It would seem there might be thin spots here, where the veil between worlds is weak.

Was Mary Howe buried alive at Newcastle's Glidden Cemetery?

The property at Jones' Corner was purchased by Robert and Patricia Geiringer in 1966. In 1995, Patricia donated eighty-six acres to the Damariscotta Lake Watershed Association (DLWA), and the house and outbuildings to the National Historic Trust for Preservation in 1997.

As of this writing, 2007, the house, while remaining protected under easement, has been sold to a private owner and is off-limits to the public. The surrounding lands belong to the DLWA. For permission to tour it, call the DLWA at 207-549-3836.

Jones Corner in Damariscotta Mills: one of Maine's 'thin spots'
where people have disappeared.

(29) Bristol

Pemaquid Point Light
Pemaquid Point Road (Route 130)

Since 1635, with the wreck of the British ship Angel Gabriel, there have been many shipwrecks on Pemaquid Point. Cries of people lost at sea have been heard on stormy nights near the lighthouse. In 1826, Congress appropriated $4,000 for the construction of a lighthouse to mark the entrances to Muscongus Bay and John Bay. The lighthouse has saved many lives since then, but it hasn't been able to save everyone. On September 16, 1903, the fishing schooner George F. Edmunds was driven into the rocks of Pemaquid Point; thirteen crewmen and the captain lost their lives. The same night, the captain of another schooner drowned at Pemaquid Point. A likeness of the Pemaquid Point Lighthouse appears on the face of Maine's commemorative quarter.

The lighthouse keeper's cottage is now the Pemaquid Point Fisherman's Museum, which opened in 1972 to showcase Maine's fishing industry. It was here that the shivering ghost of a red-haired woman wearing a shawl appeared near the fireplace as if to warm herself. Run by volunteers, the large parking lot and museum are open seven days a week from Mother's Day to Columbus Day. The lighthouse tower is open every Wednesday during the summer.

Fort William Henry
Colonial Pemaquid State Historic Site
Pemaquid River

The site of the reconstructed Fort William Henry was originally settled by the English in the 1620s. Within fifty years, its population grew to nearly that of two hundred people. In those days it was dangerous to live in any British settlement, like that of the one at Pemaquid, whose boundaries included land also claimed by the French. In 1676, the Abenakis burned the Pemaquid settlement during an uprising in King Philip's War, and a year later, the English built a two-storied, wooden fortification called Fort Charles upon the ashes of the burned settlement, but this too was destroyed in the spring of 1689.

It was replaced with Fort William Henry, which was built in 1692, and many consider this to be New England's first stone fort. Less than four years later, the French and their Native American allies destroyed it.

But before that, in February 1696, an Abenaki named Taukolexis was taken prisoner at Fort William Henry. He was in the company of several local chiefs – Abenaquid, Egremet and Toxus – walking to the fort on a mission of peace. They were interested in a prisoner exchange as well as the right to maneuver their canoes around the Point instead of the dangerous (and spirit-filled) waters of Pemaquid Point. Taukolexis was not a chief, but when his leader was unable to attend the meeting, he went in his place.

They arrived at Fort William Henry bearing a white flag, a clear indication that they didn't want a fight. During negotiations with Captain Crabb, the English attacked the Abenaki chiefs. Toxus managed to escape along with a few others, but most were killed. Taukolexis was taken prisoner. Sometimes he was taken outside and tied to a tree, but most of the time he was kept in chains inside the fort.

He died that summer. After his death, three French ships and canoes carrying a force of over two hundred Natives forced Captain Crabb's surrender. They found the body of Taukolexis and buried him on Tappan Island.

For the next thirty years, the settlement remained empty.

In 1729, Fort Frederick was built on the site of Fort William Henry by Colonel David Dunbar, who recruited around two hundred residents to live there, but his claim on the land was disputed by the Massachusetts Bay Colony. Although Fort Frederick successfully defended against several attacks, it was decommissioned in 1759. In 1775, the town of Bristol dismantled Fort Frederick during the American Revolution, lest it be reoccupied by British forces. In the 1790s, the Fort House and its accompanying barn were built. In 1902, the site was granted to the State of Maine, who reconstructed the tower and wall base six years later. In 1970, the state acquired the area that had been the village. Excavations and surveys, and their findings, performed in the 1980s and 1990s attributed to Colonial Pemaquid's dedication as a National Historic Landmark.

Many consider the Fort William Henry Memorial to be haunted. Over the years people have reported seeing a white light coming from the door of the fort and floating toward a large tree as well as the ghost of a sad man walking a foot above the ground. Many believe these manifestations may be the spirit of Taukolexis. They may also be Castine's founder and namesake, Jean-Vincent d'Abbadie, Baron of St. Castin, who is said to haunt Fort William Henry, along with the ghost of the pirate, Dixey Bull.

Bristol's Fort William Henry is the ghostly home of Taukolexis, Jean-Vincent d'Abbadie, and pirate Dixey Bull.

Also of note, skeletons believed to be those of a Native American and her baby were discovered during excavations located just outside the site of the old tavern.

Colonial Pemaquid is open to the public daily (9 a.m.-5 p.m.) from Memorial Day weekend through September 1. A day-use fee of $2 (free for children under twelve and adults over sixty-five) includes admission to the Fort William Henry Memorial, the Fort House and Museum. Driving directions: on Route 130 south in Bristol, take the Huddle Road or Snowball Hill Road (both roads go west). Follow the signs to Colonial Pemaquid.

(30) Boothbay

Haunted Hill,
Dover Road

Almost every town has a spot that makes people shiver—the hill on Dover Road in North Boothbay is no exception. This particular hill, short and quite steep, was near the old Pinkham Mill and it was here that blacksmith David and Elizabeth (nee Hutchings) Colbath made their home in 1771. In his later years, widower David Colbath was found dead one morning some distance from his house. His grievous wounds cried foul play, yet his murderer was never found. Over time, the Colbath house fell to ruins, and its cellar hole became the local haunted place where bogies were said to dwell. For over a century and a half, no one could walk past that place and not think of David Colbath's murder. According to recent reports, construction on the hill may have disturbed the "long-quiet bogies."

The Haunted Hill is on the right side of Dover Road headed north, after Twin Cove Road and before Dover Cross Road.

The Welch House Inn
56 McKown Street

According to an article in *The Boothbay Register*, when Susan Hodder and Michael Feldmann purchased the Welch House Inn in 2002, they were informed of its gentle female ghost and that several housekeepers refused to go to the third floor by themselves because objects sometimes moved and doors would open and close for inexplicable reasons. Susan and Michael hadn't been there long before they, too, encountered the strange and mysterious.

One of the first occurrences involved an antique mantle clock that had been brought to the third floor—it began to chime on the hour though it had never been wound for it needed a key, and its key had been lost a long time ago. When it chimes, sometimes its gears move and sometimes they don't. Then Susan's father, from where he stood on the back deck, watched a woman—a stranger to him—pass by several windows in succession. However, in order to walk past the last window, she would have had to go through a wall, which she apparently did, with no hesitation.

A housekeeper first saw the ghost within her first six months at the Inn. She described the ghost whom she called "Rebecca" as being in her late 20s or early 30s. Rebecca's dark blonde hair is kept in a bun or sometimes a ponytail and she wears a high-collared dress "with a pink-hued bodice." Another housekeeper is also familiar with the ghost of Rebecca who has not only been seen in Rooms 7 and 8, but has left impressions and indentations on the beds. In Room 8, Rebecca turns the radio on and it seems she prefers listening to country music. She is most active in the fall and winter months and, according to the housekeepers, she doesn't appear to everybody.

Still, it's not in her nature to frighten anyone, owners, staff or guests. Rebecca remains a gentle lady to this day. It is believed in life she may have been Rebecca Hodgdon, the daughter of Thomas Hodgdon, a man who lived at the Welch House Inn and died in 1805.

Kenniston Hill Inn Bed & Breakfast
988 Wiscasset Road

Shortly after 11 p.m. on the night of May 9, 1888, Octavia W. (Masters) Kenniston awoke to the sounds of an intruder in a room adjoining her bedroom. She quickly roused her husband, 81-year-old William, and as they were getting out of bed, the intruder sprang into the room. He struck William on the head with an iron bar, and then attacked Octavia, dealing a grievous laceration to her scalp. She fell back on the bed, but William was able to get up from the floor. As the intruder went back to the bedroom door, he turned and lit a match. Octavia could now see the intruder was a man. A white cloth with cutout eyes hid his face. William then rushed at their assailant, knocking the iron bar out of his hands and forced him into the kitchen. There, the assailant drew a butcher's knife (purchased earlier that same day). He slashed wildly inflicting several wounds upon William before breaking the blade upon the cooking stove. With the ragged edge, William was struck once more in the forehead.

The assailant threw away his broken knife and drew a revolver, firing two shots, and William went down, bleeding heavily from the knife wound to his shoulder, which had severed an artery. Octavia, presuming her husband had been shot, fled the house from a side door and ran to the home of their neighbor, Truman E. Giles. The time was 11:30 p.m. Giles called upon Dr. F. H. Crocker to attend to Octavia's head wound and then gathered some neighbors to proceed to the Kenniston house where they found William Kenniston on the kitchen floor in a pool of blood. He was dead.

William's sons, George Beaman and Albert Henry, along with his son-in-law, F.B. Greene, arrived at the Kenniston house shortly after midnight. While examining the exterior of the house by lantern-light, Greene found a timber propped up against the porch window. This was how the murderer had gotten inside—and presumably how he'd left. Greene now suspected a 19-year-old ne'er-do-well named Llewellyn Quimby, who was Octavia's son from an earlier marriage to a Boothbay man named Harvey Quimby. Harvey had died under mysterious circumstances, believed to be suicide, but many who knew him suspected he'd been murdered.

Llewellyn Quimby had lived with William and Octavia, and when he ran away from home a year earlier, he had used this same method to leave. When Llewellyn was fourteen, he'd been sent to the State Reform School for larceny, but was released on probation in 1886 at age seventeen when he contracted Typhoid fever. Upon his release, the Kennistons took him in, providing that he did chores to pay for his board. In the spring of 1887, William bought a new change of clothes for the boy and the night after receiving the clothing, Llewellyn ran away, escaping through the same window by scooting down a timber.

F.B. Greene went into the house where the neighborhood men had gathered and said, "Gentlemen, if Llewellyn Quimby is where he could do this, he is the one for us to look for." The men set off in all directions to find Quimby. Every boat in Boothbay Harbor was searched, but at 4 a.m., a black horse was discovered missing from William Kenniston's barn. A bridle had been taken as well. The horse's tracks led the search party toward Damariscotta Mills. A few miles outside Damariscotta Mills, they spotted a man upon a dark horse. Seeing someone approach, Llewellyn jumped down from the horse and ran for the woods. He was shot, receiving a grazing wound above the ear, which dazed him. He was bound by ropes and brought to the Wiscasset Jail to await trial set for October. According to his confession, after running away from the Kennistons in May 1887, he became a vagrant. He spent the winter on the wharves of Boston. In May 1888, he arrived in Rockland by steamer ship. On the night of May 8, he rowed from Barter's Island to Bath, Maine where he purchased a butcher's knife and some whiskey. Unknown to anyone, he also carried a gun. On the afternoon of May 9, he went to the Kenniston home in Boothbay Center and waited for nightfall. He then placed a 12-foot piece of timber against the windowsill of a porch window that opened into a low, unfinished room used for grain storage. Making his way through the house, he lit matches so he could see where he was going. (Charred matches had been found on the floors of several rooms.) Perhaps it had been his purpose to rob the Kennistons, but it ended in murder. Llewellyn Quimby was convicted of first-degree murder and sentenced to a life sentence in State Prison, where he died of consumption three years later.

William Kenniston had been born in Boothbay on November 9, 1806. His funeral was held at the First Congregational Church in Boothbay Center and was attended by hundreds of friends and neighbors. Reverend L. D. Evans conducted the service. Octavia Kenniston moved in with Mary Emily (Kenniston) and F.B. Greene and died January 24, 1890 at age 56, her life shortened by shattered nerves.

The Kenniston house eventually became the Kenniston Hill Inn Bed and Breakfast. It had been built by William Kenniston's father, David, as a tavern in 1786. Through the 1920s and 1930s, the inn served as a country club clubhouse. In the 1940s, it was used as a restaurant. A scrapbook kept by previous owners remains in "the Keeping Room" for guests' perusal at the Inn now owned by Jim and Geraldine Botti.

Many speculate that William Kenniston still occasionally walks the halls of his former home. In life he was an exceedingly kind and gentle man, and likewise, his ghost is far from threatening.

Boothbay Opera House
86 Townsend Avenue

The Boothbay Opera House was built in 1894. The Knights of Pythias held meetings on the second floor back when Earl 'Fingers' Cliff was the pianist and a club member. His spirit is said to haunt the Boothbay Opera House with unexplainable music wafting throughout the building since 1949. The piano has a player device attached to it, but in order for it to play by itself, the pedals must be pumped. Over the decades people have reported not only hearing— and seeing—Earl's piano play on its own, but they have also heard laughter, footsteps, voices and the muffled sounds of people talking. In November 2003, the Maine Paranormal Research Association stayed overnight to conduct research. They documented orbs and a materialized woman. The MPRA, accompanied by the New England Paranormal of Boston, returned to the Opera House in April 2005. They documented a woman on the third floor in old-fashioned clothing gazing out a window, as well as cold spots, and a military man wearing a helmet. A team representing Ghost Hunters United, a small, privately funded organization operating in New England, also investigated the Opera House in 2006 on July 29 and October 21, and their findings indicate paranormal activity taking place here. During a Dave Mallett concert, one investigator sensed a broad-shouldered shadowy man standing backstage.

Bar employees and the bar manager have witnessed the ice scoop sail from the icemaker in the liquor room, through the doorway to land on the rubber floor mat behind the bar. This has happened several times for no apparent reason. According to the bar's manager, this kind of poltergeist activity started when the scrolls were taken from the player piano and put in the liquor room. It is thought that Earl Cliff may not be pleased that the scrolls were removed from the piano.

The Ghost Hunters United team tried their best to debunk the claim of the flying ice scoop by placing it on the edge of the machine until it fell clattering to the floor. With each try, it never landed near the bar.

During their last investigation, over 1,000 photos were taken using three different cameras. Four of the photos showed something of a paranormal nature, as the image of a boy looking down from the balcony, and photos of faces taken from the third floor. Professional photographers examined the photos and could find nothing to explain the strange images.

A clarinet or oboe was heard on an EVP recording, and footsteps were heard on the second floor approaching the bar. Ghost Hunters United members believe the Opera House to be haunted, not only by the ghost of Earl Cliff, but by other spirits as well. They sensed no harmful presences.

(31) Ram Island Light
Boothbay Harbor

Ram Island is at the mouth of Boothbay Harbor. Two helpful ghosts of a man and woman warn boats away from the shoals; the woman in glowing white holds a torch over her head. She's been seen many times, always startling the boaters who see her. One fisherman reported seeing a boat on fire smashing into the rocks of Ram Island. The ghost woman was aboard the burning boat, waving him away. When he returned later to look for the boat and the woman, both were gone. According to author Robert E. Cahill, hermits living on Ram used to hang lanterns from the rocks to warn ships during storms. The ghosts of Ram Island may be a couple who lived there long before the lighthouse was built in 1883.

(32) *See Ghosts Debunked chapter*

(33) Damariscove Island
Boothbay Harbor

On the map Damariscove Island, on the outer edge of Boothbay Harbor, looks like ghostly letters spelling 'HI', reading south to north. Damariscove is where America began some four hundred years ago. It was here that America's first May Pole dance was celebrated on May 1, 1622, as documented by Phinehas Pratt, a crew member of the fishing ship, the Sparrow. "Long before Jamestown or Plymouth, Englishmen and Europeans salted fish on its shore," says Caldwell. Now Damariscove is home to ghosts.

In 1689, the island fell under attack by Native Americans. In his August 2, 1689 diary entry, John Giles tells of Captain Richard Pattishall being killed in a siege that day when his sloop was attacked in Pemaquid Harbor. Beheaded, his body was tossed into the sea, a tribute to his bravery. His remains and those of his faithful dog, who had jumped in the water after him, washed up on the shores of Damariscove. Together in the afterlife, they have haunted this island since the 1890s. The ghost dog's friendly bark has been heard many times by human ears and answered in kind by living dogs. (On a genealogical note, Captain Pattishall was the great grandfather of Patriot Paul Revere. His story is often confused with nearby Outer Heron Island where it is said a headless sea captain roams the shores searching for his missing head.)

On Damariscove, there was (and may still be) a salt-water lake reputed to be bottomless. Pirate Captain William Kidd is believed to have sunk treasures into this lake, guarding them by stringing chain across the area to hinder boats. The ghosts of Kidd's murdered crew haunt the place, protecting his loot.

Today Damariscove Island is protected by the Nature Conservancy and is owned by the Boothbay Region Land Trust. Visitors will find a small museum, hiking trails and if lucky, a ghost or two.

(34) Monhegan Island

Monhegan is located twelve miles from the mainland. More than 1,000 years ago, the Vikings, likely led by explorer Thorfinn Karlsefni, left runes carved on rocks nearby Manana Island. John Cabot charted these two islands in 1494 or 1498. Colonist John Smith visited here in May 1614. Samoset, who kindly helped the Pilgrims in 1628, had learned English from the fishermen at Monhegan. In 1698, Native Americans attacked and destroyed Monhegan's fishing fleet.

There is a cave on Monhegan that opens into the ocean. The cave is said to contain pirate treasure guarded by ghosts. The story goes that if you do find treasure here, you're not to say a word until you're out of the cave. Years ago, treasure hunters found a chest here and as they were lifting it, one of the men grunted. Immediately, ghosts snatched the chest away. Later, the cave was enlarged by dynamite. A saying went: "Dig six feet and you'll find iron; dig six more and you'll get money."

There is a female ghost on Monhegan known as The Watcher. She's said to be a blue-eyed blonde wearing a long, dark cloak and she looks seaward. She's sometimes confused with another similarly blonde-haired ghost, the girl left behind on the Isle of Shoals by Edward 'Blackbeard' Teach or Andy 'the Scot' Gordon.

Burnt Head on Monhegan was the site of a suicide in 1947. An elderly lady who lived above a gift shop leapt into the ocean from a cliff on Burnt Head and drowned. Her ghost is thought to have pushed at least one person near the ledge off the cliff and cries for help have been heard.

Monhegan Island is accessible by ferries from Port Clyde, New Harbor, and Boothbay. The museum at the Monhegan Lighthouse is open from July 1 to September 30.

(35) Wreck (False Franklin) Island
Muscongus Bay

In 1768, with no lighthouse to warn passing ships of shallow waters and perilous rocks, the Winnebec, sailing up from Boston, became lost in a winter storm and shipwrecked on False Franklin Island. She carried at least eleven souls to die slow, painful deaths in icy seas on the night of December 4. The next day, after the wind quit and the seas ran down, fishermen from the mainland found scattered debris from wreckage on nearby Cranberry and Harbor islands. Finally, they spotted what was left of the Winnebec on False Franklin. Eleven bodies lie on the shore near their doomed ship, their faces frozen in grimaces of horror.

Finding no survivors, the fishermen took the opportunity to load their boats with items from the shipwreck: chests of clothing, barrels of food and kegs of rum, not to mention valuables such as watches, jewelry and firearms. These opportunists made six trips, back and forth, and on the mainland, word was spreading about the wreck. Were those fishermen above wrenching rings from frozen fingers or pulling the boots off a corpse? Probably not—the 1700s were hard times, especially in the winter.

As they loaded their boats a seventh time, another storm sprang up, forcing the fishermen to spend the night on False Franklin in a make-shift camp constructed from broken planks from the Winnebec's hull and canvas from her sails. Sometime in the night all were awakened by intruders … a group of people with ice water dripping from their clothes, steam pouring off their bodies in a glowing vapor. They attacked the fishermen, trying to choke them to death with fingers as cold as death. The fishermen escaped, but they would never forget that terrible night.

Over the years it's been thought there may have been survivors on the wreck of the Winnebec … and they may have been murdered by the fishermen, which is why their ghosts attacked them so violently. I have to disagree. In a winter storm such as this one, with ocean temperatures near freezing, even if someone were dressed in several layers of protective wool clothing, they would only last mere minutes before hypothermia set in. Add to that a wind chill factor in the teens at best, well below zero at worst, and powerful waves dashing bodies into the rocks with no hope of rescue for hours. It's a recipe for disaster. True, some ghosts are insane and vicious, in cases of murder, suicide or a particularly painful and needless death, but sometimes ghosts lash out if they feel they've been robbed, not only of life but of their personal affects as well. (After burying their loot, pirates sometimes killed a crewman so a ghost would guard the treasure.) Did the ghosts on Wreck Island attack because they'd been shamelessly looted? Are they waiting to attack again?

Mysterious hazy lights have been spotted moving about on Wreck Island on moonlit nights—closer inspections have revealed human figures surrounded by a glowing fog near a broken hull that was swept away by the sea over two centuries ago.

(36) Stache Foods
Keene Neck Road,
Hockamock Hollow, Bremen

The former Stache Foods building is reputedly haunted by the ghost of a previous owner. This gourmet food manufacturing plant was the birthplace of the famous 'Death by Chocolate' line of products. Over the years workers have noticed faucets turning on and off by themselves, tools disappearing and then reappearing in strange places. Locals also reported seeing strange lights twinkling and flashing in the windows at night after everyone had left work, and a séance revealed the presence of a previous owner's ghost.

Knox County

(37) Warren

When examining some of the remedies and illness preventions of our forebears (such as using dead cats and sheep dung), it's a wonder we've survived this far. In 1819, a self-proclaimed doctor, John G. Lambright, moved into the Old Isley house in Warren, Maine. Among the diagnoses of patients in his care: a maggot in spinal marrow and a hair twisted around the neck of the bladder. Those are only two examples of his diagnostic 'skills.' Rather than take a patient's pulse, Lambright would study the patient's urine. Novels and history and travel books made up his 'medical library.' He believed he had the ability to transfer a patient's pain to another person. One of his 'cures' involved what he called a 'vapor bath,' and in the first five months of 1820, seven of his patients died in his house while receiving treatment. If more died before paying him, he feared going broke, so he devised a plan.

The old Isley house, now his medical clinic, used to be a tavern and it was believed to be haunted by the ghost of a murder victim. Lambright put his plan into motion, literally; doors swung open and shut in the night and strange noises began to plague the house. He also brought in a gentleman to douse the house in order to locate the murder victim's body. The rod indicated bones in the cellar, but all that was unearthed was a pile of bones, none longer than a drumstick.

Dr. Lambright wasted no time leaving town.

Among the deaths recorded in Warren in 1920: ten lost at sea, twenty-four died at sea, nine drowned, twenty died accidentally and six were suicides. Warren, Maine's strangest death may be that of Captain Lawrence Crawford.

In February 1821, Captain Crawford died in Guadaloupe, but three times before his death he saw the ghost of his English lover. The first time he saw her ghost he was in his cabin reading while his ship was docked at an Irish port. The second time he saw her while taking an evening stroll at his home in Warren. The last time he saw her was on a moonlit night; she appeared on the deck of his ship. These visitations were years apart, yet she always appeared as young and beautiful as the first time he'd met her. Captain Crawford died shortly after seeing her on his ship's deck. Was she a harbinger, a premonition of his death? Had she come for him one last time? We may never know.

(38) Marshall Point Road
Port Clyde, St. George

Built in 1832 and rebuilt in 1857, the brick and granite Marshall Point Lighthouse stands thirty feet above sea level and illuminates the entrance to Port Clyde Harbor.

Ben was the youngest son of Carl and Cora Bennett. He was his father's favorite and was often seen fishing with Carl. When Ben was twelve years old, his mother committed suicide by jumping from the town wharf and drowning herself. Ben quit school and withdrew almost completely from his father. He began hanging out with an unsavory crowd.

Late one night in the 1920s, Ben and his friends were walking down Marshall Point Road when they noticed the lights of a boat near the shore. The boys watched as men in a rowboat delivered kegs of illegal liquor to the shore near the lighthouse. One of the boys either sneezed or made some other noise that alerted the rumrunners who immediately put chase to the spying youths.

Ben Bennett's murderer haunts Marshall Point Road at Port Clyde.

One of the rumrunners, a dark-haired man wearing tall black boots, caught Ben and beheaded him with a large knife in a single blow. They tossed Ben's remains into a nearby swamp, took their illegal cache back to their boat, and were never seen again … well, not quite.

In the 1940s, a family of three was chased on Marshall Point Road by a dark-haired man with tall black boots wielding a large knife. They managed to get away, but not before realizing that his boots made no sounds as he ran.

In 1979, several people witnessed this menacing apparition, reporting that he vanished before catching up to them. Over the years many people claim to have seen the blond-haired ghost of a boy that can only be that of Ben Bennett. Sometimes he is running for his life, being chased by the knife-wielding ghost; other times, he appears in the swamp where his body was found.

Marshall Point Road is just off Drift Inn Road in Port Clyde.

---

(39) East Wind Inn
21 Mechanic Street,
Tenants Harbor, St. George

John Fuller built the East Wind Building in 1860 and rented its top floor as a Masonic Lodge until 1894. A sail loft that later became a community meeting room was on the second floor. On the first floor, John operated a mercantile, and in the basement, his sons ran a tin shop. Charles Rawley purchased the building in 1921; he renovated it as the Wan-e-set Inn. Then, Frank Scrutin purchased it in 1941, and by 1954, it was abandoned to stand vacant until 1974 when Tim Watts purchased the building, renovating it as The East Wind Inn.

The ghost of Gilbert Armstrong is thought to haunt the East Wind Inn. His shipping company, Armstrong & Keane, was nearby. This was where coaster ships were built and sold. Armstrong and his partner established a fleet of their own to haul lime and paving blocks, but by 1874 all seven of their ships had been lost at sea. Construction of their eighth ship stopped and the business went bankrupt. Gilbert's partner, Harry Keane, went to work at a shipyard in Camden. Crestfallen, Gilbert went to work in the East Wind Building mercantile … and it is said he remains here to this day.

Ghosts of Sarah H. Meservey and Gilbert Armstrong haunt the East Wind Inn in Tenants Harbor.

Gilbert Armstrong's sad specter has been seen materializing on the main staircase. Some, who cannot see him, have heard his footsteps on the stairs. Gilbert may be lonely, but he isn't alone.

In Rooms 12 and 14, which are now one unit, guests have told of being pinned to their beds by a ghost woman. Other guests on the third floor reported hearing cries at around 3 a.m. They sensed cold spots that move about the room. Awakened by loud footsteps, the owner of the inn got out of bed to check the lobby. No one was there—but the swinging dining room door was moving as if somebody had just entered.

The third floor, according to psychic Annika Hurwitt, seems haunted by a woman who was strangled to death. That was just what happened to 37-year-old Sarah H. Meservey on December 22, 1877, while her husband, Captain Luther Meservey, was away at sea. Throughout the October 1878 murder trial, Nathan F. Hart proclaimed himself innocent of first-degree murder. He was guilty, though. (He'd been put on trial for "talking too much," describing how he dreamed Sarah had been strangled before her body was found.)

Thinking no one was home, Hart had entered the Meservey home with the intent to rob; he slipped into the kitchen by raising the unlocked window. He was going through the kitchen closet when Sarah Meservey returned home. She and he struggled and upset the kitchen table. In the midst of their wrestling, her scarf became entangled, tightened and she fell to the floor gasping for air and clawing at her neck. Hart stepped back, watching her, and making no move to help her, he ran off. The only thing that could save his hide was if Sarah was dead. This is what he told his own wife.

As soon as evening fell, Nathan Hart and his wife walked until they could see the Meservey house. The lights were off; the place was dark. They climbed in through the kitchen window and found Sarah on the floor. To make it appear that a robber had killed her, they tied Sarah's hands behind her back and ransacked the house.

Nathan's wife quickly jotted out a threatening note, supposedly from someone who hated Sarah and wished her harm. The note was left, crumpled, beside the body.

The court convicted Nathan Hart of first-degree murder. His wife lived unsuspected, even hailed for her suffering, for Nathan never mentioned her involvement. He died in a prison cell in Thomaston, Maine. Everyone in Tenants Harbor attended his funeral, including at least two people who knew he wasn't guilty of first-degree murder: his wife and his lawyer who finally revealed the true story of what happened to Sarah Meservey fifty years later.

(40) Keag Store
4 Elm Street
South Thomaston

Built in 1854, the Keag Store took its name from a shortened form of the Abenaki name Wessaweskeag. The second floor of the store was considered haunted when it was run as an inn years ago—people reported seeing a dark, shadowy figure upstairs, but no one knew anything about the origins of the ghost.

(41) Matinicus Rock Light
Matinicus Isle Plantation

Almost every child on the Eastern Seaboard is familiar with the story of Abbie Burgess, the brave young lady who tended the Matinicus Light by herself during a terrible January storm in 1856. Few adults know about the lighthouse keeper of an earlier time who hung himself in the tower and no one noticed until several evenings passed when the beacon remained unlit. (A child's grave on the island is that of Bessie Grant, who died in 1878. She was the niece of Abbie Burgess Grant, mentioned above. Bessie's father, John Francis Grant, was the lighthouse keeper until 1890.)

The first lighthouse on Matinicus was actually two wooden towers built in 1827. In 1848, granite towers replaced the wooden ones. A fog bell was added nine years later (and can be seen at the Maine Lighthouse Museum in Rockland). A steam-driven whistle replaced it in 1869, the first of its kind to be used anywhere.

When the United States Coast Guard took over maintaining the light, they weren't told that part of the original dwelling might be haunted, although the door to the keeper's dwelling was kept locked for just that reason. It wasn't long before that door was unlocked.

As soon as the door was opened, Coast Guardsmen tending the lighthouse reported poltergeist activity: doors banging shut, cups flying off tables, cupboard doors that kept opening, light bulbs frequently burning out, and perhaps worst of all, the beacon light shutting off for no apparent reason. When the door was locked again, the phenomena died down. During inspection, the door was re-opened—and the phenomena began almost immediately. Before the commanding officer left Matinicus, he ordered that door to be closed and kept shut.

Matinicus Island can be reached by water taxis from Rockland (which also offer puffin-sighting trips) and by the Maine State Ferry Service operating year-round out of Rockland. For rates, dates and times of departure check online at *www.maine.gov/mdot/ferry* or call 1-800-491-4883.

---

(42) Owls Head Light

Owls Head Lighthouse, at the entrance to Rockland Harbor, was built in 1825. The keeper's house was built in 1854 with a generator building and an oil house built in 1895. According to the 2006 October issue of *Coastal Living*, Owls Head Light is indeed haunted by the ghosts of a former keeper and an old woman. Over the years, keepers have nicknamed her "Little Lady." They say the ghostly keeper is a frugal soul; he insists that the thermostats be turned down. He also polishes the brass of the Fresnel lens. His footprints have been seen and heard in the tower—as well as being seen on the grounds after a snowfall. He has been seen—and befriended—by at least one child. The domain of the "Little Lady" is the kitchen; she sometimes rattles the silverware. Neither ghost is threatening; they appear to be doing in the afterlife just what they'd done in life.

Owls Head Light State Park, the parking lot and park grounds are open to the public. The Lighthouse and keepers house belong to the U.S. Coast Guard and are not open to the public, however, that's not to say a ghost cannot be seen or detected on the grounds.

"Little Lady" and an old lighthouse keeper haunt Owls Head Light.

(43) Thompson Community Center
51 Union Road, Union

The Thompson Community Center was named after Union-born Moxie® inventor, Dr. Augustin Thompson (11/25/1835-6/8/1903) in Union. (Since the late 1800s to 1906, the soft drink Moxie® was advertised as a nerve tonic, a digestive aid and stimulant, although according to its 1885 trademark, it was intended to "cure paralysis, softening of the brain, mental imbecility" among other illnesses.)

The building was originally a school and gym, and now serves as home to a museum, a Boy Scout Troop, Lifeflight Emergency Medical Service, and a food pantry. Concerts and dances are held in the gym. Over the years, volunteers at the center have reported seeing the ghost of a cigar-smoking man dressed in 1920s attire. He appears in the gym and after he vanishes, the scents of his cigar smoke and cologne linger in the air.

The bathroom on the second floor is also said to be haunted by the ghost of a woman who sometimes screams for help. When this happens, the bathroom door slams shut and "shakes violently" before swinging open again. Allegedly, two rapes occurred in this bathroom in the 1930s.

In the classroom directly below the second floor bathroom, a menacing "dark" man has materialized; he chased a volunteer into another room; doors have opened and closed on their own; and disembodied voices have been heard in the hallways.

(44) Rockland

Lime Rock Inn
96 Limerock Street

The LimeRock Inn was built in 1890 as a private residence for Congressman Charles E. Littlefield. The mirror in the hallway was a gift to his bride. In 1949, the house was purchased by Dr. Oren Lawry, who operated his medical practice there. The Grand Manan room was once his examining room. Dr. Lawry retired and sold the home in 1994 and the house was transformed into Rockland Historic District's first bed and breakfast.

The presences of ghosts have been experienced by many, whom over the years have reported giggling spirits of children at the top of the stairs. Some ghosts are content to wait in the front parlor that once served as a waiting room. They have been seen gazing out the windows. All are friendly and peaceful and are said to welcome guests in search of friendly spirits.

Captain Lindsey House
5 Lindsey Street

Members of the Paranormal Association of Maine have visited the Captain Lindsey House and claim the inn is haunted by as many as thirty-six spirits, including previous owners Captain Lindsey and T. B. Severence.

For fourteen British pounds, Captain George Lindsey's father purchased a sizeable tract of land in Rockland. In 1832, the Lindsey House was built and within five years, it became an inn with a livery stable and tavern. In 1857, he sold the inn to T. B. Severence. It remained an inn until 1924 when the Camden-Rockland Water Company bought the property and utilized its rooms for offices and laboratories. In 1994, the Water Company moved out and in 1995, it was sold to Captain Ken and Ellen Barnes who lovingly restored the inn to its former glory.

A proud spirit named Ensign also occupies The Captain Lindsey House. Five-year-old Jeffrey and his four-year-old sister Emmy are there too, awaiting the return of their father. Most paranormal activity occurs in the parlor and consists of moving water glasses and doors opening and closing.

The Captain Lindsey House, located in the heart of the Historic Waterfront District, is thought to be Rockland's oldest inn—a warm and beautiful place to stay for spirits as well as the living.

Berry Manor Inn,
81 Talbot Avenue

Listed on the National Registry of Historic Places, the Berry Manor Inn was built in 1898 as a wedding gift from Charles H. Berry to his new bride. Charles Berry was a merchant and nephew of the Civil War General, Hiram Berry. The grand house served as a primary residence for four generations of Berrys. In 1998, the present owners transformed the house to an inn, making certain that all renovations met the standards of the Department of the Interior to ensure that the original architecture was preserved.

Guests have reported ghosts greeting them through the windows. According to the innkeepers, guests sensitive to the presence of ghosts experience a warm feeling of tranquility at Berry Manor Inn.

(45) Goose River Bridge
Route 1, Rockport

The Town of Goose River, now Rockport, fought against British raids during the American Revolution. William Richardson was a Patriot living in Goose River. When Commodore Samuel Tucker, a privateer, captured an English East Indiaman ship, he hired Richardson to guide his ship to Harpswell so the loot could be unloaded and hidden. Because of Richardson's help in eluding the Redcoats, Commodore Tucker was able to sail safely onward to Salem, Massachusetts.

In 1793 the Treaty of Paris was signed, ending the war with Britain, and Goose River's citizens began to celebrate. The grandest party in town was hosted by William Richardson, who kept the ale flowing by making rounds with a pitcher in each hand. Sometime during the party, William wandered off, happily drunk, singing and dancing his way around town until he came to the Goose River Bridge. Here, he was met by three men on horseback, and not realizing they were British, he cheerily offered them ale from his pitchers in celebration of the American victory.

William was struck in the head with the butt of a rifle and left to die on the bridge.

For over two hundred years, William Richardson's ghost, nicknamed 'Pitcher Man,' has been seen and heard on Route 1 on the bridge that crosses Goose River. Witnesses tell of him thrusting his pitcher into open car windows or approaching vehicles, holding his pitchers out, only to vanish. He has also been seen in the wooded areas near the bridge. One could say he's always in fine spirits.

(46) Maiden's Cliff
Mt. Megunticook Trail
Camden Hills State Park

Camden was the filming location for the movies Peyton Place and Casper, and it is not without its own ghost. Mt. Megunticook is the highest of the Camden Hills at 1,100 feet in elevation, but it's relatively easy to climb. The large white cross at Maiden's Cliff marks the tragedy of May 7, 1864, when 12-year-old Eleanora French fell to her death.

According to a 1915 article in *The Camden Herald*, Zadoc French, his wife and their twelve children lived at Lincolnville Beach. On May 7, 1864, two of the French children accompanied their schoolteacher, Miss Hartshorn, and friend Randall Young in hiking up Mt. Megunticook from the Lincolnville side.

Upon reaching the top, Randall announced that they were upon the "boldest cliff on the rock," and he proceeded to find a large rock to roll over the cliff's edge. Miss Hartshorn and the younger French girl sat down while Eleanora "rambled around" them. Then a gust of wind blew Eleanora's hat from her head. Eleanora managed to find its net and sat on a rock near the edge of the cliff to put it on. The younger sister turned to say something to her schoolteacher, but was interrupted by a sudden scream. She looked back to where Eleanora had been sitting on the rock, but she was gone.

As fast as he could, Randall Young climbed the 300-foot drop on the face of the cliff to the place where Eleanora landed. Remarkably, she survived the fall. Help arrived and the young girl was rescued. Around 12:30 a.m. that night, Eleanora died at home, despite not suffering a single broken bone. It is believed she succumbed to internal injuries.

Camden resident and inventor of duplex telegraphy, Joseph B. Stearns, erected the first cross a few years after Eleanora's death; it was replaced around 1947. The new cross blew down January 17, 1980. Its replacement weighed six hundred pounds and was erected with the help of the Air National Guard. Laite Funeral Home donated the monument that's at the foot of the cross, which reads: In memory of Eleanora French.

Eleanora's ghost has been seen playing on the cliff from which she fell. Some claim to have seen a girl's old-fashioned hat taken by wind, tumbling down the face of the cliff, followed by the distant sounds of screams.

The Maiden Cliff trailhead is on Route 52, two miles from the intersection with Route 1 in Camden. Parking is available above the beach on Lake Megunticook. Be prepared for a good hike on a marked trail. It's considered bad luck to take anything, including flowers, from Maiden Cliff.

Waldo County

(47) Belfast

Pitcher Cemetery
Pitcher Road (off Route 3)

Often mistakenly called Pine Wood Cemetery in online descriptions, Belfast's Pitcher Cemetery is home to more than twenty-six resting souls. Graves date back to 1831. For years, photographs taken here have shown the presence of orbs. Occasionally, while driving on Pitcher Road, people have claimed that someone or something banged on their car doors and fenders. There have also been reports of footsteps appearing in the grass as if somebody was walking, but no one appears to be there. In the folklore section of his book, Tom Seymour tells of a buggy wheel that supposedly crosses Pitcher Road near the cemetery every Halloween at midnight. According to the story, a young woman was riding home in her buggy one Halloween night in the 1870s, but when she reached Pitcher Cemetery, her horse shied and bolted. The wheel on her buggy broke away from its axle and she was killed in the wreck.

Her name may have been either Vera or Elvira, and some believe she may have been a witch. Every Halloween at midnight, people have gathered near Pitcher Cemetery in hopes of witnessing a 'phantom wheel' that flies across the road—or to catch a glimpse of her ghost.

People gather at Belfast's Pitcher Cemetery on Halloween to witness a phantom wheel and a witch's ghost.

(48) 1794 Watchtide™
Bed and Breakfast...by the Sea,
190 West Main Street, Searsport
www.watchtide.com

Six craftsmen worked together to build the Watchtide as well as many of the big, captain's capes along Main Street in Searsport, a town then known as Prospect. The Watchtide was built for Brigadier General Henry Knox, Secretary of War under President George Washington and the founder of West Point. After General Knox sold it, the property went through several owners, mostly sea captains, in the heyday of great sailing ships.

In the early 1900s, George and Rose Pettee of Egremont, Massachusetts bought it as a summer cottage and in 1917, their daughter, Francis, and three of her friends opened a teahouse called the 'College T House,' which eventually became the 'College Club Inn.' Former First Lady Eleanor Roosevelt made the College Club Inn a favorite stop on her way to her and Franklin's summer cottage in Campobello. The College Club Inn lasted until World War II, when it became a private home.

Nancy-Linn Nellis and Jack Elliot purchased it in 1994. They planned to bring the property back to its former glory as an Inn, but they hadn't been told that ghosts were included in the sale. One morning in April 1994, Nancy-Linn saw a woman standing in the dining room and assumed she was a friend who'd come to visit. After exchanging a few pleasantries, Nancy walked into the kitchen. Her friend joined her a half hour later. The friend had no knowledge of being in the dining room, looking at the Winslow Homer painting on the wall or speaking to Nancy earlier that morning. The women thought this very odd, but after conducting some research on their own, they discovered Nancy had probably encountered the ghost of Connie Banks, a former owner who died in the house. She was described as having short, bobbed hair and was wearing a long, old-fashioned type jacket.

Several ghosts haunt this former sea captain's Searsport home, the 1794 Watchtide Bed and Breakfast...by the Sea. *Courtesy of Lora Lee Gray.*

During her research, a previous owner admitted to Nancy that he sometimes found toilet paper unrolled and strewn across floors and small pools of water, a little over an inch in diameter, on the floor of the library beneath chairs. Were these 'presents' left by the ghost of a pet cat or dog?

Over the years guests have reported seeing a man with light-colored hair and woman dressed in old-style clothes standing at the foot of their beds. These ghosts—and others—seem to prefer the English Garden Room; they also like music. The second story became notorious for radios that turned on for no reason at all at various times of the night, even in unoccupied rooms.

During renovations, Nancy and Jack sometimes heard loud, unexplainable rumbling sounds, so Nancy placed angelic figures in every room and that seemed to calm the ghosts. She also sold angel figures in her adjoining shop, Angels to Antiques, but no matter how careful she was to lock the doors in the evening, she'd return the next day to find them unlocked.

Nancy and Jack retired in 2006 and sold the Watchtide to Patricia and Frank Kulla. The 1794 WatchtideTM Bed and Breakfast...by the Sea is proudly listed on the National Register of Historic Places.

(49) The Hichborn Inn
Church Street
Stockton Springs

The beautiful Italianate Victorian was originally built as a home for shipbuilder Nathan Griffin Hichborn; Captain K. Waldmer Dahl later purchased it. Shortly after moving in, the present owners became aware that they weren't they only ones living here. Certainly, the house made a number of strange noises, but that was to be expected. The first real clue that they weren't alone occurred before any restorations were made.

The family was about to leave for the day when "a deafening crash" came from the dining room. They rushed back to find a mirror lying on the floor … and an iron that had been left plugged in was on. The family believes the spirits who live here intervened to prevent a house fire that might have otherwise occurred.

They have also witnessed a helium balloon moving through the rooms as if being tugged along by an unseen hand.

One of the spirits at the Hichborn Inn may be that of Harriet Hichborn, daughter of Nathan Griffin Hichborn. It is said she suffered a nervous breakdown after the suicide of her fiancé and was admitted to a mental hospital.

Singing has been heard coming from the area near the piano in the front hallway where sometimes stray notes are played with no one sitting there, and other times, according to a neighbor, entire songs composed by Bela Bartok have emanated from the instrument. (Mary Hichborn used to play the piano and Bartok's music was popular during her life.)

Guests have reported seeing the ghost of a man standing at the upstairs window, gazing out to sea. He has been identified as Captain K. Waldmer Dahl and has been known to walk straight through walls.

Phantom smells occasionally waft through the inn: the fragrances of old-fashioned perfume and the warm scent of a meal cooking (when no one's working in the kitchen). To learn more about the ghosts residing at the Hichborn Inn, you really should schedule a visit.

(50) Prospect

Fort Knox

This Fort Knox in Prospect, Maine bears no relation to the mint in Kentucky, although both were named after Major General Henry Knox, the first American Secretary of War. There is no gold bullion in the Maine fort; it was built in the mid-1800s to protect the Penobscot River. (Stephen King fans will recognize the Penobscot as the river running through Derry, Maine.) Judging from photographs taken by the North East Paranormal Society, a good, old-fashioned haunting cannot be ruled out. During one psychic group's overnight vigil at the fort in 2004, several people in the party heard and saw things they couldn't explain. It spooked some of them. It isn't odd that ghost stories are the best selling books at the fort's gift shop.

The fort itself is shaped like a pentagon with five evenly spaced corners. Conspiracy theorists and psychics alike believe in the power of material shape and a pentagon is considered one of the oldest and most 'energetic' architectural styles, only a step or two below a pyramid. The fort hasn't been structurally altered much since it was first built; it's chiefly comprised of granite, which contains a good amount of quartz crystal shards that glitter in the sunlight—many believe crystal is an excellent conductor for energies from another plane.

There are ghostly tales of soldiers from the Civil War era still occupying Fort Knox; on occasion they've been sighted or footsteps have been heard, as well as the firing of rifles and cannons, even though no battle was fought at the fort. Such stories began shortly after the military stopped using the fort. Nowadays, with high tech video equipment and digital cameras, orbs are commonly picked up in various spots. There are so many dark nooks and crannies, it would seem almost impossible not to see an apparition, however every ghost hunter must bear in mind how easy it is to be fooled by their own imaginations.

If you have a chance to go to the Psychic/Paranormal Faire held every August at the fort, by all means go—you'll have a great time and can make a family day out of it, too.

Items to bring with you: a bottle of drinking water, a camera (digital if you have one), flashlight, and spending money. Be sure to wear comfy footwear with sturdy treads. All these things are good, but the best thing you can bring is an open mind tempered with logic and commonsense. In addition, if, by some chance, the hair stands up on the back of your neck and you break out in goose bumps—or you see or hear something unexplainable, or you are physically touched by something chilly and ethereal, count yourself among the lucky for the experience! Over 50,000 visitors explore Fort Knox annually. General admission is free for those younger than five or older than 65, $3 for ages 12 to 64, $1 for children 5 to 11. Additional donations are suggested for a few attractions. The fort is open daily 8:30 a.m. through sunset, May 1 through Nov. 1, with optional guided tours available seven days a week. Group tours also can be arranged. The Fort Knox State Historic Site is administered by the Maine Department of Conservation and is managed by Maine's Bureau of Parks and Lands.

Spirits of Civil War soldiers haunt Fort Knox in Prospect. *Courtesy of Lora Lee Gray.*

Penobscot River

In the late 1700s, Samuel Griffin (1728-1800) of Prospect was fishing with his sons Elisha and Eben when the three looked up to see two old-style ships attacking one another nearby. Although it was a bit foggy, they identified the vessels as true pirate ships—but the age of piracy was well over by the mid-1700s. In amazement, the fishermen watched the pirates clamber aboard the other's ship to fight with swords. They saw and heard enough to know the fighting was genuine. Then it was over almost as quickly as it had started. The fog lifted and with it both pirate ships vanished as if they'd never been there. This shook the Griffins so deeply that they gave up fishing for the day and went home.

Pirates did indeed sail up the Penobscot River in the early 1700s. They'd taken a brig off Sandy Point and slew every passenger aboard. Bodies washed ashore but not withstanding the stench of rotting corpses, they were quickly buried in a sandbar. Most didn't stay buried long for before floating to the surface. Not too long ago, human bones, blanched white and worn smooth by sand and sea, were found along the shores.

(51) The Fountain House
44 Main Street, Winterport

Built in the mid-1800s, the Fountain House is one of Winterport's oldest houses. It was a sea captain's home, belonging to Captain John Atwood. In the 1920s, James Foley opened the Foley & Son Funeral Home; it closed its doors in 1992.

Now it's a pub and restaurant, owned by Rick Glencross and Jennifer Murphy, who originally intended to downplay the funeral home part of the house's history but something changed their minds. "...Odd things happened," according to Jenny. It started with sounds of footsteps and voices talking in empty rooms, then lights turned on and off by themselves, and objects missing would turn up again in unexpected places.

In a December 20, 2006 article in the *Bangor Daily News*, Rick described a "luminescent woman" who walked past him one night while he was having supper. He refers to her as "Mehetabel." She didn't look at him, just walked on by as if he wasn't there. On another occasion, a waitress reported hearing footsteps, then felt someone breathe on the back of her neck. She quickly turned, but no one was there. Over the years, residents and guests of the Foley house have reported hearing sounds of heavy footsteps on the back stairs ... but upon checking, no one was there.

Even so, Jenny and Rick don't feel there's anything frightening at the house/restaurant. Nothing flies around, no goo bleeds from the walls and no one tells them to get out. Their unique restaurant features a Haunted Pub complete with a wicker viewing casket and posters of Herman Munster, Casper the Friendly Ghost, and Elvira, Mistress of the Dark among others. People of any age would be right at home and it's nice to see a house that once served the dead now serving the living with great food, good company, and live music—not to mention the spirits. For reservations at the Fountain House, call 207-223-4051.

The Fountain House, a former funeral home turned pub in Winterport.

Buck's Monument, Silver Lake Cemetery, Lake Alamoostook, Fort George, Castine Village, Deer Isle, The Lucerne Inn, The Black House, Criterion Theater, The Bar Harbor Inn, The Ledgelawn Inn, Somes Sound, Swans Island, Crocker House Inn, Sullivan Harbor, Gouldsboro, Town Pier, Schoodic Island, Prospect Harbor Light, Catherine's Hill

(52) Bucksport

Buck's Monument
Main Street

Jonathan Buck was born February 20, 1719 in Woburn, Massachusetts. He grew up in Haverhill and became a commander at Fort Pownal in Stockton Springs on what was then the Maine frontier. During the American Revolution, Buck became Colonel of the 5th Militia Regiment of Lincoln County. He was forced to flee to the safety of Bucksport; from there, he traveled by land to Haverhill, Massachusetts. He never forgot Maine, though. After the war, he returned to Maine and founded the settlement of Bucksport. He became a Justice of the Peace before his death in March 1795.

In 1852, fifty-seven years after his death, Colonel Buck's descendants erected a monument near his grave on Oak Hill ... and about fifty years after that, stories about him began to circulate, for on the face of the stone, clearly visible from Main Street, is a large mark that resembles a human leg and ends in a pointed foot.

In 1902, the September issue of *The New England Magazine* published a story by J. O. Whittmore titled "The Witch's Curse, a Legend of an Old Maine Town," which discredits the stories circulating about Colonel Buck and the leg on his monument. (He ends with saying "...the legend was made to fit the foot and not the foot to fit the witch's curse.") However, this did little to quell the rumors that persist to this day.

One of the rumors describes Colonel Buck seeking the aid of a Native American medicine woman who went by the Franco-Christianized name of Jacquelyn. She tended to some of his men who were sick or injured and when she asked for payment, Buck had none to give. She then put a curse on him and he in turn accused her of witchcraft and saw that she was put to death.

Another version of the story concerns a condemned witch named Ann Harraway who swore to "dance upon Buck's grave." Some versions paint her as the mother of Buck's illegitimate son. In the lovechild versions, Ann is burned at the stake and the son runs off with a piece of her leg. Another strange stain on Buck's monument looks somewhat like a heart, hence this legend created to include an illicit love affair.

The problem with the witch's curse lies in the period in which the events supposedly occurred. The last legalized executions for condemned witches ended in 1692 in Salem, Massachusetts and were long over by the mid-to-late 1700s. In Colonial America, there are no records of witches being burnt at the stake. They were killed by hanging; one was pressed to death beneath stones, and several died in prison while awaiting their executions.

Maine certainly had ties to the Salem witch-hunt, but no records exist of anyone being accused of witchcraft and executed in Maine.

Supposedly, Colonel Buck's heirs have had the front of the monument sanded and cleaned, but like any good curse, it just keeps coming back. Author Thomas A. Verde asks why the masons who cut the stone didn't notice the flaw right away. Why would Buck's

This "leg-shaped" inclusion has inspired tales about Bucksport's
founder for over 150 years. *Courtesy of Tom Gray.*

descendants buy a stone with such an odd fault on its face? More over, why would they keep it?

My guess is only that the flaw, known to stone masons as an inclusion, probably started out as a light stain which grew darker as time went on … and by the time anyone thought of replacing the stone, stories about Colonel Buck were already in circulation. Over the years people from all over the world have journeyed to Bucksport to see the leg on the stone. It's been a boon for the tourist trade, that's for certain.

The leg on Buck's monument faces Route 1, easily viewed from the shopping center parking lot across the road. For those who want a closer look, they can read the plaque near the monument stating that Colonel Buck was "an honorable, industrious man," as well as being a Patriot and founder of Bucksport.

Bucksport's Oak Hill Cemetery. Jonathan Buck's monument is the tallest stone facing Route 1. *Courtesy of Lora Lee Gray.*

Silver Lake Cemetery
Silver Lake Road

Finding Silver Lake Road is a little tricky. Go north on Bucksport's Main Street, driving past the intersection to Verona Island (as if you were going to the paper mill) and take McDonald Street on the right. McDonald Street eventually becomes a dirt road known as Silver Lake Road. The cemetery is on the right. The road and cemetery are both said to be haunted by the ghost of Sarah 'Sally' Ware, a murder victim who wanders this area on foggy autumn nights.

On October 2, 1898, a woman's decomposed and mutilated body was found in the brush in a pasture near Miles Lane (present-day Bucksport High School parking lot). She was identified as 52-year-old Sarah Ware. Her left ear had been severed with the area of skull in front of the ear extending to the cheekbone missing. Parts of her upper and lower jaws had been hacked away, along with her lips. (Some of these parts were found near the body.) She'd been raped. When her body was moved for transport to the morgue, her head fell off. It was put in a box and taken for evidence in a murder trial that convicted and later acquitted William T. Treworgy of her murder. After the trial, Ware's skull was stored in the Ellsworth Courthouse safe until it was laid to rest with her body almost one hundred years later. Her body is believed to have been buried in the pauper's section of the Silver Lake Cemetery.

In 1930, part of the Silver Lake Cemetery was moved to make way for a reservoir, and some have speculated that Sarah's grave was overlooked during the relocation ... hence the reason she haunts the graveyard; others say she's searching for her missing head.

Nearly a century after Sarah Ware's murder, a Bucksport woman began having nightmares of a faceless woman with dirty blonde hair and an old-fashioned dress, trapped underwater, crying out for help. With the research assistance of author Carol Schulte, it is believed the woman haunting her dreams was none other than Sarah Ware. Bucksport Librarian Ed Spooner has done extensive research on this unsolved murder.

The ghost of murder victim Sarah Ware haunts Silver Lake Road and cemetery in Bucksport. *Courtesy of Lora Lee Gray.*

(53) Lake Alamoostook
Route 1, East Orland

East Orland is best known for its Craig Brook National Fish Hatchery. Operating since the late 1800s, Craig Brook is America's oldest Atlantic salmon hatchery. Around the time the fish hatchery started, a vacationing Bostonian invited his pregnant girlfriend out for a relaxing night of romance at Lake Alamostook. He suggested a moonlit canoe ride and to this she was quite agreeable. When they reached the middle of the lake, he took up his paddle, and gave her a strange look, one she'd never seen on his face until now. Romance was the furthest thing from his mind—as he began striking her on the side of the head with the paddle, intent on murder. She screamed, trying to fend off his blows, but he knocked her unconscious. The canoe tipped over when he dumped her body overboard.

He couldn't swim, so to save himself he clung to the overturned canoe, hoping someone would hear his pleas for help. No one answered his shouts except the loons—he could hear them laughing all around him. Minutes stretched into long hours, and still they laughed. In his mind, he believed they were laughing at him for getting into such a predicament. He'd meant to kill his girlfriend so he wouldn't have to marry her … but now it looked like the tables had been turned in a twist of cruel irony. The loons were the only witnesses to his crime and no matter how much he yelled, they wouldn't stop laughing. In the morning, he was rescued … but he was not the same young man who'd paddled out to the middle of the lake the night before.

Now he was a raving lunatic unable to suppress his own laughter, laughing himself to the point of tears, giggling uncontrollably—even when he was arrested for murder. After serving two years behind bars, he committed suicide by biting off his tongue and letting himself bleed to death. For years after, both prisoners and guards swore they heard his eerie lunatic laughter coming from that jail cell …

and at Lake Alamoostook, when you hear the laughter of loons, listen carefully for the unnerving sounds of manic glee that continue to haunt the lake. Some people have seen a strange shadow in the shape of a giant loon flying over the lake. Some claim it's the ghost of the murderer—others think it's a spirit of nature that made certain justice would be served. The picnic area at Alamoostook Lake is open daily from 6 a.m. to sunset.

(54) Castine

Fort George, Wadsworth Cove Road

"A drummer was killed, the night of the skirmish, at the battery near Bank's house, and, for a good many years after, people used to say that they could hear his ghost drumming there at midnight." William Hutchings of Penobscot narrated this tale to Joseph L. Stevens, Jr. in August 1855. Aaron Banks, who owned the house near the battery, lived at Majabigwaduce (now Castine). His wife Mary was a cousin of the Hutchings family. William Hutchings was 14 years old at the time of this skirmish. (He was the next to last oldest survivor among American Revolution veterans.)

According to the Wilson Museum Bulletin, the drummer was killed in battle on an August night in 1779 when British troops held the peninsula of Castine. It is thought that the drummer's ghost eventually moved from the Banks battery to the remains of nearby Fort George, which had been an impressive structure, newly built the year he was killed. In the southwest corner of the fort's ruins, an entrance leads to a small, underground room lined with bricks, likely the original dungeon of the fort where the drummer's ghost is said to have taken residence. This has inspired some rather imaginative stories over the years.

One such invention (circa 1876) was that the drummer was a young American boy who'd been imprisoned by the British in the dungeon and left to die when they abandoned the fort. In September

1882, Noah Brooks gave yet another account of the drummer in his article 'An Old Town with a History', published in *The Century Magazine*. Apparently, the drummer was left to die when the British evacuated Castine in 1814. When the dungeon of the fort was opened years later, a skeleton was found with a drum by its side. In 1943, Katharine Butler Hathaway's *The Little Locksmith*, published by Coward-McCann, told of an imprisoned 14-year-old drummer who drummed steadily for three weeks every year, starting in the last week of August. According to Tom Seymour in his 2003 book *Tom Seymour's Maine: A Maine Anthology* Hancock County's first official hanging occurred at Fort George, and at dusk in the summer, the ghost of the drummer can be heard tapping out a death march.

The drummer is without doubt Castine's most famous ghost. His name and age has been lost to history; we don't know if he was American or British, although it makes sense that if he'd been on the side of the Maine militia, William Hutchins would have stated his name. William's peer, a boy surnamed Trask, played the fife and merited a mention. If the drummer were a Maine boy, would his ghost haunt a fort built by the British? Why not return home?

At any rate, whether British or American, young or middle aged, one fact is not disputed: that's the haunted sound of his midnight drumming in August ... and the beat goes on.

The ruins at Fort George are located just off Battle Avenue in Castine. Fort George is open year round and the admission is free.

Castine village

In the village of Castine, where the old Tilden & Co. store later stood, the Joseph Perkins family once had their home. In the cellar of the Perkins home there was an old stone oven. Once a week, it was the custom of Mrs. Perkins to do her baking in this oven. She had hired a Penobscot Native woman as a servant, and this servant used the old oven as a cradle for her little "papoose." One day after putting the infant down for a nap, the servant left the house, and Mrs. Perkins came home and built a fire in the stove, unaware of the babe sleeping within its baking chamber. It was said that for a long while after folks could hear an eerie, tiny voice squeaking in infantile Penobscot and ever since then, the cellar area has been haunted.

(55) Deer Isle

Just before the American Revolution, Chief Swunksus lived on Deer Isle and was willing to split the island with his friend, a Boston man named Conary. Conary, though, wanted the entire island for himself and challenged Swunksus that the next time they met, they would fight to the death and the victor would have full possession of the island. Swunksus returned to his half of the island to bide his time and ambush Conary—but he found a whiskey jug instead. After drinking his fill of the firewater, he passed out, forgetting all about Conary's challenge.

It was here that Conary found him, snoring loudly, and the empty whiskey jug beside him. Conary shot him in the head with his musket and claimed ownership of the entire island. That was not to be the end of the murdered Swunksus, though, for the chief has been seen walking the beaches of Deer Isle at night. In the woods, the sound of his loud snoring has been heard in broad daylight.

(56) The Lucerne Inn
2517 Main Road
Lucerne-in-Maine, Dedham

The Lucerne Inn began as 'the Lake House' for the John Phillips family, original settlers of Dedham. Due to its location on the old stagecoach route, it became a tavern known as 'the Half Way House' in 1814, a rest stop between Bangor and Ellsworth. The railroad winding through Dedham in the 1890s brought travelers to Lucerne-in-Maine from as far away as Boston and New York City. In 1925 Harold Saddlemire bought the Half Way House and its surrounding land, which he called Lucerne, "the Switzerland of America," after Lucerne, Switzerland. Overlooking picturesque Phillips Lake, nestled in the foothills of Bald Mountain, the Lucerne Inn is listed on the National Register of Historic Places.

In the 1920s, the land surrounding Lucerne Inn was destined as one of America's first "planned communities," and the village of Lucerne was established in 1927. Because of the Great Depression, the planned community never materialized.

The Lucerne Inn is located across from the Lucerne Hills Golf Club, a classic course designed by Donald Ross. It's a 9-hole green featuring hills topped with bent Province grass. Over the years the colonial gabled inn has expanded to include rooms with fireplaces, whirlpool tubs and views overlooking the lake . . . and so too, have its ghost stories.

Tales of ghosts at Lucerne Inn have been circulating for years. In the early 1900s, a caretaker named Sam caught his wife cheating on him with a guest in Room 8. He shot them both before killing himself. His ghost is believed to turn lights on and off, and is to blame for the occasional objects taking flight into the air. Guests have also seen human shadows moving on walls in empty rooms. Unexplainable thumping noises have been heard, and according to some, the furniture in Room 8 is occasionally moved when no one has been in the room. Guests and employees have reported hearing the voices of a woman and young child talking in the hall near Room 8, accompanied by the sounds of footsteps. The ghost of Sam remains a gentleman; no matter how distraught, he has never harmed a guest.

A ghostly family stays at the Lucerne Inn in Dedham.

(57) The Black House
Woodlawn Museum,
172 Surry Road, Ellsworth

The Black House at Woodlawn in Ellsworth originally belonged to Colonel John Black, who owned three hundred acres, and built his fortune in lumber. Architect Asher Benjamin built the estate in four years, 1824-1828. It served as a home to the Black family for three generations. George Nixon Black, Jr. left Woodlawn in his will to the Hancock County Trustees of Public Reservations stipulating that it must never be used as a residence. It has been open to the public since 1930. In 1969, it was registered on the National Register of Historic Places.

Born in London in 1781, John Black was a clerk for General David Cobb, who owned great tracts of land in Maine Territory, which was the last frontier of New England and then part of the Massachusetts Bay Colony. John Black came to Gouldsborough (now Gouldsboro) in 1799; and in 1802, he married General Cobb's daughter, Mary. They moved to Ellsworth in 1810, and in the War of 1812, John Black became a colonel in the Massachusetts Militia. He was a well-liked, intelligent, honest man. After the war, he helped launch Maine's lumber industry. Upon his death, an 1856 article in the Ellsworth American claimed his was "probably the largest estate ever left by any person in the state east of Portland."

At Woodlawn, visitors are stepping back in time—the mansion with all its original furnishings and decor provides a glimpse into what life was like for a wealthy family in the 1800s. Not only can people tour the house museum, they can walk through the formal gardens and along the lily pond, have a picnic on the lawn. They can also hike, jog or ski the trails Colonel Black built as exercise tracks for his horses. A side trail, designated by granite pillars, leads to where the Blacks are buried.

Many visitors have remarked about feeling a benign, male presence in the Black House. Evidently, the spirit residing here doesn't mind strangers walking through the estate. He's not so lenient with the staff, however—if they're not out of the house by 6 p.m., he's been known to knock chairs over and sometimes slams the door shut behind the last person to leave. Some have seen candlelight through the windows, after the place has been locked for the night.

Schedule of tours at the Black House: May - Tuesday thru Sunday, 1-4 p.m.; June thru September: Tuesday to Saturday, 10 a.m. to 5 p.m.; Sundays, 1-4 p.m. and October - Tuesday thru Sunday, 1-4 p.m. Admission for adults is $7.50, children, $3 (under age 5 free); hours and admission fees are updated at the website: www.woodlawn.com. The public park at Woodlawn is open year round from sunset to sunrise, no fees.

A male ghost keeps the staff in line at the Black House in Ellsworth.

(58) Bar Harbor

Criterion Theater
35 Cottage Street

The Criterion Theater was built in 1932 by George McKay, who went all out with an art deco interior, an unsupported flying balcony, intercoms, central vacuuming, and tangerine velvet curtains. The McKay family owned the Criterion for thirty-five years before selling it to Peter Morison, son of naval historian Samuel Eliot Morison. When Peter died, he left the Criterion to his wife, Betty "B.J." Morison, who was a mystery novelist in her own right. She is remembered for her raspy voice and her thin cigarettes that she smoked in elegantly long holders. She is also remembered for collecting tickets in the foyer and for making every moviegoer remove their chewing gum. Some speculate that her ghost still visits the Criterion from time to time.

A ghost glowing in green flames was seen backstage by a man who was cleaning late one night, but this had happened while B.J. Morrison was still alive. During the 1930s prohibition, the Criterion was home to a speakeasy housed beneath the stage. Stories have circulated for years about the secret tunnels under the older streets of Bar Harbor that were used by rumrunners. Perhaps something happened in the speakeasy or in a nearby tunnel to cause the visible manifestation of a disturbed ghost?

The Bar Harbor Inn
Reading Room Restaurant
Newport Drive

The Mount Desert Reading Room was incorporated in 1887 to promote "literary and social culture." It was designed by William Randolph Emerson. In 1910 President Taft was entertained there during a stay in Bar Harbor. In 1921 it was open to the public and featured a restaurant; a year later it was sold to the Maine Central Railroad. During World War II, the Navy leased the building as observation headquarters; and during the "Fire of 1947", which burned nearly three-quarters of Mount Desert Island, the American Red Cross used the building to give shelter and assistance to those in need.

In 1950, a forty-room wing of the Hotel Bar Harbor was built, followed by a twenty-room motel ten years later. In 1987, David J. Witham purchased the property and changed the name to the Bar Harbor Inn. It now has one hundred and fifty-three guest rooms and modern amenities.

The Bar Harbor Inn is home to no less than three ghosts. One is a lady who wears a long cloak. She's been seen most often at dusk on the path near the shore and she looks seaward as if expecting her lover's return. Two male ghosts inhabit the Reading Room Restaurant. They are impeccably dressed in Victorian suits and have been seen sitting by the window.

The Ledgelawn Inn
66 Mt. Desert Street

Constructed in 1904 by Bar Harbor carpenter John Clark as a summer cottage for John Brigham, a wealthy and well-heeled shoe manufacturer from Massachusetts, the Ledgelawn Inn has been called the "grande dame" of Bar Harbor's Historic Corridor. It was built on the ashes of the old Shannon estate. Architect Fred Savage designed the house in Victorian Rusticator (Colonial Revival) style ... the Brighams were known to host lavish parties in the early 1900s. Nearly all of the Ledgelawn's furnishings are originals that once belonged to the John Brigham family. The Ledgelawn was first established as a commercial property in the 1970s, purchased by Nancy Cloud and Michael Miles, who owned it for over twenty years before selling to Joan and Daniel Mills who have been working on preserving and restoring its rich historic elegance.

The Ledgelawn Inn is home to a ghost called 'the lady in white.' Seen by many, some believe she may have been John Brigham's daughter. Another ghost is Katherine, who died here; she haunts the Ledgelawn's third floor. There is also some speculation that John Brigham himself never really left his home and still walks the halls.

There is a certain room that seems always "occupied" by a presence. Over the years guests have reported mirrors moved by an unseen force in this room, as well the tactile sensations of being touched, disembodied voices and orbs. The ghosts here are friendly and not to be feared.

(59) Somes Sound, Route 102, Fernald Point, Southwest Harbor

The first French mission in North America was established in 1613 at Fernald Point on Somes Sound in Southwest Harbor. At Saint Saviour Mission, on land granted to Sieur de Poutrincourt, the French Jesuits were starting to build a fort, sow their gardens and baptize the Natives when the unexpected happened.

An English ship commanded by Captain Samuel Argall sailed into Somes Sound. The crewmen attacked the mission, killing two missionaries surnamed Birard and Masse (who'd been living in the area since 1609) and mortally wounding Priest Gilbert du Thet. Half of the survivors were sent away in a small ship. The other half was taken to Jamestown in the Virginia Territory where they expected to be put to death.

Captain Argall was ordered to take them back to Saint Saviour Mission, but they found passage back to France, perhaps on a fishing boat.

The spirits of Birard, Masse and Gilbert du Thet are believed to haunt the pool just around the corner from Valley Cove at Fernald Point. On spring nights, many have heard the voices of men praying in French, sometimes accompanied by the rhythmic splashing of oars.

Two French missionaries and a Jesuit priest have haunted Fernald Cove in Somes Sound since 1613.

(60) Swans Island

Swans Island's oldest human inhabitants were the Abenakis; clamshell mounds left by them are still there today. It was charted by Samuel Champlain in 1604, and was named for Colonel James Swan, a Scotsman, soldier, writer, merchant and politician. He took part in the Boston Tea Party and fought in the Battle of Bunker Hill in the American Revolution. He was a friend of Lafayette, Knox and George Washington, and purchased this island, along with twenty-four other islands, in 1784 … but as much as he wanted to, he never lived here. He died and was buried in Paris, France. Swans Island's first white settler was Revolutionary War veteran David Smith, a former New Hampshire man, who moved here in 1791.

Just off the coast from Brooklin and Tremont, and comprised of two islands, Swans Island has a year-round community of approximately three hundred and fifty hearty souls as well as around seven hundred summer residents. It also has its share of ghosts, according to Judith W. Monroe's book *Peripheral Visions*. Tales are told of strange faces illuminated by an eerie and otherworldly fire glowing in the night on the road to Hockamock Head.

At Ghost Hollow, in the northwest corner of Minturn, where Lily Pond Stream flows down to an inlet in Burntcoat Harbor, a woman has been seen at low tide, walking the mudflats. She wears a bright red dress and carries a baby bundled in her arms. Those who've seen her aren't aware they've seen a ghost until she disappears, leaving footprints in the mud that end abruptly. She is thought to be the ghost of a young woman whose body washed ashore during high tide a week after she went missing. She was pregnant at the time of her death.

The mudflats of Ghost Hollow are home to at least two more apparitions: a young couple, teenage lovers, whose parents tried to put an end to their romance. They went missing one night, but strangely, they didn't take a boat, and after a long while, they were presumed dead. Their specters have been seen on moon-drenched nights as they walk hand-in-hand at low tide.

At Mackerel Cove, the voice of a young wife from the 1800s has been heard calling out to her husband, telling him she hears something. They were in a rowboat on their way to nearby Orono Island for a honeymoon picnic when the fog shut in. Her last words were a warning, for their boat was crushed seconds later by a steamship ferry. On foggy days, her ghost still calls out, apparently still certain she hears danger coming through the mist.

Swans Island's villages are: Atlantic at Mackerel Cove near the ferry landing, Swans Island Village at Burntcoat Harbor, and Minturn (across the harbor from the Village). Visitors arrive by ferry from Bass Harbor. There arc no stores, but there's plenty else to be enjoyed. The Harbor Watch Motel has bike and kayak rentals. There are also Beds & Breakfasts, and a berth of house rentals. Visit Seaside Hall Museum (admission free) at Mackerel Cove for exhibits of island life and history. The Library is housed in the old Atlantic schoolhouse near The Lobster & Marine Museum and the Natural History Museum (all are near the ferry dock). Fine Sand Beach at Toothacher Cove is best enjoyed at low tide for wading and swimming. If low tide comes in the evening, make haste to Ghost Hollow … you never know who you'll see there.

Swans Island can be reached by the Maine State Ferry Service operating year-round out of Bass Harbor. For rates, dates and times of departure, check online at www.maine.gov/mdot/ferry or call 1-800-491-4883.

(61) Crocker House Inn
967 Point Road,
Hancock Point

Built in 1886 by Jones and Harriett Kelley, the Crocker House served as a boardinghouse until they sold the property to Julius H. Crocker on September 30, 1901. Josephine Kief bought the inn in 1921 and sold it in 1928 to Isma Bryant, who sold it in 1948 to Guy Riegel. The Inn went to Dezso Szabo in 1969, who sold it to artist William Moise and a group of his friends in 1976. (Moise worked as a private secretary for Dr. Wilhelm Reich and married Reich's daughter, Eva.) In 1980, Richard Malaby, the current owner, bought the Crocker House Inn.

For decades, the inn served travelers arriving off the Maine Central Railroad or the Hancock Point-Bar Harbor Ferry. In its heyday before the Great Depression, there were seventy restaurants and fifty-five inns on Hancock Point.

The Baroness was a flamboyant character, a beautiful Hungarian who immigrated to New York in 1918. She became a burlesque dancer and first married Baron Carl Lanoff, then later Guy Riegel. At the inn she always referred to herself as 'Baroness Olga Lanoff,' a title from her first marriage. In Argentina, she became a tea production entrepreneur, and developed her own blend. (Every room in the Crocker House displays a box of the Baroness's Bol-Yerba Tea).

Stories abound of her gala dinner parties where she sometimes fan-danced atop tables for her guests. A dark-eyed beauty with a quick smile and flirtatious laugh, it isn't hard to imagine that she never really left the Inn … especially since she's been seen by both staff and guests over the years. "The Baroness was something of a scandal…" Richard Malaby says, "her ghost haunts the inn."

The ghost of Baroness Olga Lanoff occasionally entertains visitors at the Crocker House in Hancock.

Mike Merritt, who has worked at the Crocker House for years, says he's been around "when books have swooped off the bookshelf." Guests have reported towels hanging in the bathroom suddenly waving like flags in the wind, and faucets turned on by unseen hands.

The Crocker House is located at 967 Point Road in Hancock, approximately 4.8 miles from Route 1. It is open year round.

(62) Sullivan Harbor

John Cling was a clock and watch repairman in the late 1800s, peddling his trade from Bar Harbor to Calais. He'd come to Maine on a barque loaded with salt from Liverpool, England, and almost immediately questions and rumors abounded about this unique stranger. If he had paid a dear sum for the voyage to America, why did he bunk with the crew? Had he committed a terrible crime back in London? Was he hiding from the law? Some said he hailed from a wealthy noble family, that Cling was a Lord's son who'd murdered his sweetheart. The speculations went on and on ... however no one in Maine was notified to be on the lookout for anyone matching John Cling's description. Because of his unusual appearance, he would have been difficult to miss.

Cling let everyone know he was highly educated and he truly preferred speaking only with educated men. He traveled his route on long wooden stilts and carried the tools of his trade in an old salt bag. While he walked, his tin utensils would jangle and clang, hence his nickname: Old Cling Clang. It was said you could hear him coming a half a mile away. Not wanting to scare animals, whenever he met a horse pulling a buggy or a team of oxen pulling a wagon, he always stopped by the roadside and waited until they passed. Cling had a cocker spaniel that followed him wherever he went. When she had pups, he carried them in another salt bag, stopping every so often to let them feed. He never slept in a bed, but carried with him a barrelhead that served as his chair and pillow, and he used salt bags for bedding (which he washed everyday in salt water, little matter if it was seventy degrees outside or thirty below zero). His home was an old overturned boat on Sullivan's shore. He never received mail nor did he send out letters.

Cling was deathly afraid of roosters and ran screaming whenever he heard a rooster crow at daybreak. Any other time of the day was fine, but a rooster crowing at dawn drove him stark raving crazy. He fashioned his clothing out of salt and grain bags and went barefoot until it snowed. Then he made boots out of bags. Some thought he might have lived like this as some sort of self-denial penance for misdeeds. This became apparent the winter day he came running out from under his boat, shrieking. Later, folks found out he was on a hunger strike. He never explained why he denied himself food, only that he'd had a terrible nightmare that reminded him of some obligatory self-punishment. He never begged or asked for anything, but had to be invited to take a meal or to come inside and take shelter from a storm. One bitterly cold night, John Cling froze to death beneath his boat with only a few salt bags to cover himself. Where he is buried is anyone's guess as the Sullivan town records were destroyed by fire.

A Sullivan Harbor lady was doing dishes at her kitchen sink when she heard a noise in her hall stairway. Upon investigation she saw the grey form of a man. "We both kind of froze for a second," she said. Then the form turned and went down the stairs. She knew immediately it was John Cling; he'd died one hundred and thirty years before on her property.

Apparently, he's still around—if you're in Sullivan, or any of the coastal towns between Calais and Bar Harbor, turn an ear to the wind. You just might hear the chiming, jangling sounds of Cling's spirit as he makes his rounds in death as he did in life.

(63) Gouldsboro

On the afternoon of October 19, 1961, a fisherman driving along Route 1 near Gouldsboro reported seeing a large four-engine plane fly across the road at an altitude of around six hundred feet and disappear behind a ridge a mile or so away. The plane should have reappeared—but it didn't—and nor did it crash—although over fifty people in the area reported seeing and/or hearing the low-flying craft.

Officials from Dow Air Force Base in Bangor searched the area by ground and helicopter, but no wreckage was found. No airline was missing a plane on that date in this area. The search was called off that evening when an eyewitness description of a partial tail number matched up with a two-engine patrol aircraft at Brunswick Naval Air Station. What exactly had people seen and heard? A phantom plane? No one really knows.

(64) Winter Harbor

Town Pier
Harbor Road

I've asked local fishermen if they know anything about the following story, but everyone I asked has never heard of it. The story goes like this: during the American Revolution, some deserters from the armies of both the Americans and British formed a rowdy gang of rogues called 'the Harbour Boys.' At night, navigating their rowboats toward the lantern-lit windows of homes along the shores, these ruffians assaulted several small settlements of Downeast Maine. They pillaged, raped and plundered, leaving nothing but ashes in their wake.

Winter Harbor's original name was Musquito (Mosquito) Harbor when it was part of Gouldsborough Plantation No. 3. Gouldsboro became incorporated as a town in 1789. Winter Harbor separated from Gouldsboro to become a town in 1895.

In the days of the American Revolution, a few settlers lived in Musquito Harbor, but suspecting they were soon to be raided by the Harbour Boys, the settlers formed a plan to protect their homes: they agreed to light no candles or lanterns in their houses that night and instead set lit lanterns on the rocks along the harbor.

That particular night was windy and moonless as the Harbour Boys neared the lights of Winter Harbor in their rowboats. When they saw that they were headed at full speed straight into jagged rocks, it was too late to turn away and their boats were smashed. Every one of the Harbour Boys drowned that night.

According to the story, on wind-driven, moonless nights, the cries of their ghosts can be heard over the breaking surf. "Row, boys, row for your lives!" Perhaps their spirits are condemned to relive their final, fateful night repeatedly for eternity.

I may be mistaken, but I believe this story actually refers to the Biddeford Pool area, which was called Winter Harbor since the early 1600s. Biddeford's Winter Harbor had a considerably larger population base at the time of the American Revolution than did the Winter Harbor in southern Hancock County. Fort Mary (later replaced by Fort John Hill) had been built in 'Winter Harbor' in 1708 and in 1718, this settlement became the town of Biddeford, which is now Maine's southernmost city.

Town pier, Winter Harbor.

(64) Schoodic Island

Part of Acadia National Park, Schoodic Island is a small islet across the reach from Blueberry Hill and the Devil's Anvil. From a distance, it looks inviting, a good place for a picnic or to relax after kayaking. Appearances, however, can be deceiving. What looks like grass between the shore and the trees are actually thick hedges of thorn bushes. If you manage to get past the thorns, you'd find the footing tricky. What appears smooth and gentle is soft and spongy, very uneven—the perfect habitat for yellow jackets and the sea birds that nest here, but not for anything – or anyone – else.

A long time ago, an enterprising soul set about digging a hole on the island in hopes of finding pirate loot. As his shovel struck the top of a sea chest with brass hinges, he heard a low groan and seawater filled the hole. He went back to the mainland for help in retrieving the chest, but was unable to locate the hole he'd dug.

Some people claim the ground on this island "moves." 'Grave Tree' stands at the north end of the island, a sole, ancient tree that, in recent years, has given up the ghost. Its stump stands grey and gnarled, a silent testament to death. In 1895, the corpse of a red-haired woman clad in a nightgown washed up on Schoodic Island. Because no one knew her name or whereabouts, she was buried beneath Grave Tree. Her grave marker, however, is never seen in the same spot twice.

(65) Prospect Harbor Light

The first lighthouse in Prospect Harbor was built in 1850. In 1891, a 38-foot tall wooden conical tower with a keeper's house, which later became known as Gull Cottage, replaced the granite lighthouse.

Gull Cottage is said to be haunted by the ghost of Captain Workman, father of John Workman, the last lighthouse keeper who lived there until 1953, even though the light was automated in 1934. John's father died in the cottage while lighting his pipe, and many people report smelling pipe smoke. Guests also tell of hearing footsteps at night and of seeing lights turn on and off as well as human-shaped shadows on the walls of empty rooms.

On a windowsill above the stairs that leads to the second story, three statuettes of ocean farers are turned to face the sea ... but some nights the middle statuette, the captain in the dark wool coat, turns around to face the stairs. This could easily be explained away if not for the window being so difficult to reach.

On 'Haunted Lighthouses,' a 1998 Cold Spot documentary on The Learning Channel, lighthouse historian Jeremy D'Entremont told of an entry in the guest book from a family who stayed at Gull Cottage. While putting a son to bed, the boy looked past his father and asked, "Who are you?" The father turned around, but no one was there.

There have been sightings of a boy and girl who drowned in the early 1900s; they've been seen playing on the rocks near the lighthouse.

My mother-in-law, Elsie Gray, worked at Gull Cottage in the mid-1900s, tending to the children of the doctor who lived there. She believed it was haunted because of some unusual occurrences she witnessed, for instance: pipe smoke in rooms where no one had been smoking.

The lighthouse tower is now owned by the Coast Guard; Gull Cottage is owned by the Navy and is available, year-round, for rent to current and retired Navy Personnel. It sleeps up to six and reservations can be made for two to five nights with preference to active military. Reservations are only taken between 8 a.m. and 11 a.m. on the first working day of the month, and the reservation must be made for the following month. (For example, if you want to rent Gull Cottage in June, call in May.) The number to call is: 207-963-7700.

Once every August during the Winter Harbor Lobster Festival, the Navy hosts an open house for everyone (military and civilians) at the Prospect Harbor Lighthouse. The lighthouse is easily seen from Main Street, Route 186, in Prospect Harbor, across from Stintson's Canning.

(66) Catherine's Hill,
Blackswoods (Black Wood) Road,
Township 10 (T10SD)

Providing a shorter alternative than Route 1 from Franklin to Cherryfield, Blackswoods Road (Route 182) winds 12.5 miles through the hills near Spring River and Tunk Lake as a Maine Scenic Highway. Catherine's Hill (960 feet in elevation, a.k.a. Catherine Mountain in the Maine Atlas and Gazetteer) is said to be the easternmost point in the U.S. to receive good cell phone reception. The Black Wood Road on Catherine's Hill is also known by locals as one of Maine's most haunted areas. According to the BSBPM: tales are still told of "mysterious visions" from the crest of Catherine's Hill. Lifelong Franklin resident and friend, historian Bruce Carter, mentions the "mystery lady of Black Woods" in his book Oblivion & Dead Relatives Downeast. He goes on to say that there was a dance hall atop Catherine's Hill in the 1930s.

The dance hall fits well with the ghost story. It was perhaps leaving this dance hall one night that a young lady named Catherine Black lost her life in a tragic car accident. The young man driving the car was said to have died in the crash that decapitated Catherine. Since the 1930s, her ghost has been seen by many walking along the roadside near the hill named after her. Some see her as a glowing lady in a white dress and claim she's looking for her boyfriend. Some drivers said she's flagged them down for a ride and mentions that her car is wrecked, however, they see no sign of a car accident. Those who give her a ride are shocked when she disappears into thin air, usually just after cresting Catherine's Hill. Other drivers see her as a decapitated corpse standing by the road and can only guess that she's searching for her lost head. The Parkers, who owned a house on the outskirts of Franklin, had a mysterious visitor in the late 1920s … a young woman in a white dress knocked on their front door and said her car had been wrecked. They bade her to come inside from the cold and warm herself by the fireplace—and she did, only to disappear moments later.

A view of Catherine's Hill from Fox Pond.

According to The Mystery Network, Catherine was on her way home from a formal event in Ellsworth in the early 1970s when her car crashed into a tree at the summit of the hill and because no one stopped to help her, she died of exposure. This version of the story doesn't fit the period; the earliest Catherine stories have been circulating since the late 1920s and early 30s. It doesn't fit Maine people either. If anyone had noticed the wreckage of her car, they certainly would have stopped to help. That's the way Mainers are. Lastly, there are no records in the state archives of any deaths in the Black Woods in the 1970s. Still, there are plenty of strange occurrences in the Black Woods.

In the 1960s, on a warm spring day, a 15-year-old accompanied his grandfather fishing at Tunk Lake. However as young lads in spring are wont to do, he wished a little more action than Tunk was producing. So up over the hill Wesley climbed, staying on the main highway until he was abreast of an old cabin. Being the curious type, he ventured nearer to the side of the cabin, enough so he could take a peek through the open and un-shuttered windows. The interior was dusty and from the looks of it, no one had lived there in quite some time. Seeing nothing of interest, he continued his trek over the hill, down the other side for a ways and followed a path to Spring River Lake. Here he stayed until he remembered Gramps lunch bucket and a few goodies contained therein. Back up over the hill, Wesley trudged. He thought to himself, one last inspection of the old cabin was in order. This he did, only to discover all the ragged curtains had been pulled closed. Yet the building had appeared empty and not lived in for some time. Wesley wasted no time leaving the scene. He was glad to make contact with Gramps and his lunch pail.

One summer night in 1946/47 around 9:30 p.m., a Franklin couple was returning home after seeing a movie at Milbridge Theater. Near the summit of Catherine's Hill, they noticed a young lady walking by the side of the road. After World War II there was very little traffic, so they stopped to ask if she needed a ride. She accepted and sat between the couple in their pickup truck. The older lady noticed that young stranger felt cold. The night was warm, but she was wearing a filmy white dress. When asked, she said the cold didn't bother her. When asked where she was going or where she'd been, the stranger's answers were evasive. They traveled ten miles to the couple's farmhouse on a lonely side road. Since it was late, they asked the young lady to stay the night and they would help her in the morning to be on her way. The couple retired upstairs to their bedroom, but not before providing warm bedding to their guest so she could sleep comfortably on the sofa. Around midnight, the couple was awakened by a very loud noise from downstairs. They hurried to the kitchen to find all the pots and pans strewn around the kitchen and pantry floor. There was no sign of the young lady. They searched every room of the farmhouse. Strangely, all the doors remained locked from the inside. The next day, the couple asked around town if anyone had seen a young woman in a white dress in the area, but it seemed she'd disappeared without a trace.

At night, the Black Woods take on an entirely different persona. Just traveling the road may raise goose bumps on your arms as well as raise the hairs on the nape of your neck. You'll know you're being watched … and by chance, you just might spot the one who's watching you; she'll be walking at the side of the road, a breeze rippling through her luminescent dancing gown.

Catherine's Hill can be reached from the junction of Routes 182 and 200 in Franklin. Drive east on Route 182 for 9.6 miles. There is room for parking in a small turnout near an open meadow. If you follow the trail west, you can hike the mile up to Catherine's Hill by following markers. If going during the day, do not stray from the trails—in the early 1900s there were several mining operations in this area and some of the mineshafts have not been filled in. From the crest of Catherine's Hill, you'll have a breathtaking view of Tunk Lake to the southeast and Spring River Lake to the northeast.

The unmistakable ghost of Tall Barney has been seen for over a century on Beals Island.

Washington County

Tall Barney, Prophesy Rock, Round Lake area, Bad Little Falls, Machiasport, Passamaquoddy Bay, The Lubec Light office building, Pocock Island

(67) Tall Barney,
Jonesport & Beals Island

Tall Barney's real name was Barnabas Coffin Beal, III, and his is the rather large ghost of a lobsterman seen by many in the Jonesport/Beals area over the last century. He was born December 13, 1835, the son of Beal's Island's first settler. A kindred spirit to Bangor's lumberjack Paul Bunyon, Barney was "bigger than life," a man of remarkable stature standing around 6'7" and weighing in the neighborhood of three hundred pounds. According to those who've seen his ghost since his death on February 1, 1899, Tall Barney hasn't gotten any smaller. Because of his great strength and confidence, he was known as 'the Cock of the Walk' from Cape Elizabeth to Lubec, and stories of his exploits circulated to Canada after English sailors attempted to board his fishing boat at Grand Manan, New Brunswick. According to the tales, Tall Barney broke their guns over his knee and sent the sailors packing. In Rockland, he allegedly stopped a runaway horse with a single blow from his fist. (Some sources say this happened in Portland, and Barney "hauled off and thumped the horse," killing the animal instantly because he didn't like the policeman riding him.) He could easily carry two barrels of flour or two kegs of beer, one tucked under each arm, and he won a prizefight in Boston.

Tall Barney's Restaurant at 52 Main Street in Jonesport has a "liars' table," where local fishermen sit and would never think of fabricating a story or two about the size of a fish they've caught (wink, wink).

Tall Barney's Restaurant in Jonesport, just before Beals Island bridge.

(68) Prophesy Rock,
Kilton Point, Jonesboro

Jonesboro, Maine is home to at least two American Revolution heroines. Hannah Weston, who is remembered for carrying ammunition sixteen miles on foot through the woods to Machias to supply Patriots who'd captured the British ship Margaretta, and Nell Kilton, a prophetess who met her end by a hangman's noose in Canada.

Nell is one of Maine's oldest ghosts. In 1740, she and her widowed father moved from Plymouth, Massachusetts to Jonesboro, Maine, where they quickly made friends with the Native Passamaquoddies who lived in the area at the time. Nell taught school and her father worked as a trapper.

For Nell, friendship with a certain Passamaquoddy boy developed into love. They were to be married, but her father wouldn't hear of it. She could trade with the Indians; she could be a friend to them and she could teach them, but he wasn't about to stand for her marrying one of them. Outraged, he murdered Nell's beau with an axe, and despite Nell's frenetic pleas and protests, scalped the boy. Then he tossed Nell from his household and warned her never to return.

As an outcast, Nell made her living as a translator between the English, French and Passamaquoddies. She also taught school in both Canada and Maine. Somewhere along the line, she picked up the talent of foretelling the future, especially when it came to matters of war.

In 1755, when the British drove the French Acadians from Nova Scotia, Nell Kilton urged the Passamaquoddies to be especially kind to the French. (Like many colonists, she resented the increasing taxes and trade restrictions England demanded.) In 1775, she returned to Jonesboro to warn her former townspeople of an upcoming war between the American colonies and Britain. She foretold the Battle of Lexington and the British surrender at Yorktown.

Nell was captured by the British, who never forgave her for her part in the French and Indian Wars. She was hung as a spy in St. John, New Brunswick, Canada on March 1, 1777. Before her death on the gallows, her last words were a vow to return to 'Prophesy Rock' at Kilton Point in Jonesboro on the anniversary of her death, to warn her people of war whenever it threatened America. Her ghost appeared there on March 1 prior to the War of 1812; also, the Mexican Conflict in 1846. She appeared before the start of the American Civil War in 1861, the Spanish-American War of 1898 and World War I in 1917. According to Ariel, she also predicted World War II, the Korean War, the Vietnam War and the Persian Gulf War.

The easiest way to view Prophesy Rock is to turn right from Route 1 in Jonesboro onto Roques Bluff Road, then take the first right onto the Evergreen Point Road. Go to the second boat landing (it's the one at the end of the road) and you'll see Prophesy Rock on Kilton's Point directly across the water.

Beyond the lobster boats lies Prophesy Rock at Kilton's Point in Jonesboro.

(69) Round Lake area, Township 18

According to *100 Little Ghastly Ghost Stories*, "In a wood in Maine ... on stormy nights, an airplane falls and splinters noiselessly among the somber trees." No doubt, the authors refer to the ghost of L'Oiseau Blanc, the White Bird, a French airplane, which if ever found, will be hailed as the aircraft that made the first transatlantic crossing. Leaving Le Bouget airfield near Paris, the White Bird was piloted by Charles Nungesser and navigated by Francois Coli. The plane was sighted sixteen times in Newfoundland (airplanes were a rarity in that place and time). On the morning of May 9, 1927, government telephone operator Julia Day heard a plane in the distance from her office in Old Perlican, Newfoundland, Canada. At 9:20 a.m., Arthur Doyle saw "a white airplane coming off the Atlantic Bacalieu," and his report is backed by three eyewitnesses. Seven people reported seeing an airplane pass north of Harbor Grace just before 10 a.m. Mainer Anson Berry reported hearing a low-flying plane crash near his camp at Round Lake in the late afternoon of May 9, 1927. He said that just before the crash, the plane's engine sounded "erratic." Experts concur that the White Bird would have been low on fuel at this point in its flight.

In the Levasseur bi-wing powered by a 450 hp Lorraine-Dietrich 12-cylinder, water-cooled engine, Nungesser and Coli planned to fly from Paris to New York twelve days before Charles Lindberg set off to make his own historic flight. They were ace pilots; Nungesser had shot down forty-three German planes while serving in France's Service Aeronautique and Coli had piloted a long distance flight to Africa. Just under the open cockpit, the White Bird was decorated with Nungesser's World War I insignia of a large black heart containing two candles burning, and a coffin over a skull and crossbones.

In 1980, the mystery of the White Bird's disappearance caught the attention of writer-researcher Gunnar Hansen (probably best remembered among horror fans as Leatherface from the Texas

Chainsaw Massacre), who spoke with a hunter who claimed that in 1950, he discovered an old engine partially buried in the ground near the area where Anson Berry heard a plane crash. Over the years, several parties, including NUMA (National Underwater and Marine Agency) led by author Clive Cussler, have combed the area in the hills of Round Lake and have turned up small pieces of struts and parts of an engine not manufactured in the U.S. or Canada. During a logging operation in 1974, however, locals described "a really big motor" that was dragged out of the woods and hauled away for salvage. If that's the case, then the White Bird has likely been lost to history ... still, it stands to reason that Nungesser's gold teeth, the metal plate in his head and the surgical pins holding his appendages together would show up in the general vicinity of the crash. (He'd broken both legs and several other bones during an earlier crash.) According to Charles Lindbergh in his book, The Spirit of St. Louis, Nungesser and Coli vanished "like midnight ghosts."

The 1999 movie 'Restless Spirits' tells the tale of the daughter of a dead airplane pilot who visits her grandmother in Newfoundland and encounters the ghosts of Nungesser and Coli who are doomed to repeatedly relive their crash into a nearby pond. Although initially made for young teens, the depiction of Nungesser and the White Bird in Restless Spirits is eerily unswerving in accurate historical detail. Perhaps the movie is the basis for sightings of the White Bird's ghost ... but then again, maybe not.

In recent years, several campers in the area have heard what sounded like a "very low-flying aircraft" and at least two people have seen treetops parting and water splashing as if being zoomed over by a small plane—but no plane was seen in the area. This occurred on the late afternoon of a windless, sunny day that happened to be the anniversary of the White Bird's crash.

Round Lake is due northeast of Route 192 in Northfield. The area is boggy before you get to the hills and the underbrush is dense. Hiking in this area isn't easy, but well worth it if you find a piece of the White Bird or encounter its ghost.

(70) Bad Little Falls, Machias

The Whiddah was a 300-ton former slave ship belonging to Sam Bellamy. As a pirate ship, she was armed with twenty-eight guns (small canons). On April 27, 1717, she sank on a sandbar near Wellfleet, Massachusetts during a storm. Captain Bellamy went down with his ship along with at least one hundred and thirty-seven members of his crew.

In June 1984, Barry Clifford and his diving crew found the *Whiddah* and its treasure of more than 30,000 pounds sterling, ivory, gold and indigo. Clifford later founded the museum in Provincetown, Massachusetts, which contains artifacts from the wrecked *Whiddah*.

Pirate Sam Bellamy built a fort at the Bad Little Falls in Machias.
Courtesy of Bob Gray.

The Bad Little Falls in the heart of Machias on Route 1 is very close to where Sam Bellamy had set up camp and is known to locals as 'the old pirate fort'. He intended it as a place where pirates like him could live in relative safety and seclusion. He died before realizing his dream. Throughout the years, many youngsters have walked along the banks of the Machias River in search of pirate loot left behind.

The ghost ship of the Whiddah has been seen off the coast of Machias and Machiasport.

An example of the 'bad' in Bad Little Falls—the roar of the water is almost deafening. *Courtesy of Bob Gray.*

(71) Machiasport

Machias is a town of firsts: the first naval battle of the American Revolution was fought in the waters off Machias on June 12, 1775, when the British warship, Margaretta, was captured. (Ballast stones from the Margaretta were used to build the fireplace of the Porter Memorial Library.) Machias is also home of the first authentic recorded American haunting. (These events occurred while Machiasport was still part of the town of Machias.)

Nelly Hooper, daughter of David Hooper of Machias, was married to George Butler, but she and her unborn child died in childbirth in 1799. Apparently, before she died, George promised never to remarry if something were to happen to her. When he fell in love with Lydia Blasdell shortly after Nelly died, strange noises occurred in the Blasdell house, the loudest noted on August 9, 1799.

Nelly Hooper Butler's ghost appeared to over two hundred witnesses at Machiasport. *Courtesy of Bob Gray.*

On January 2, 1800, a disembodied female voice was heard in the Blasdell home, identifying herself as the late Nelly Hooper Butler. The ghost requested that Captain Abner Blasdell send for her father, David, and her husband, George. Captain Blasdell succeeded in bringing David Hooper to his cellar.

Hooper asked the ghost questions that only Nelly could answer. He later wrote, "I believe it was her voice. She gave such clear and irresistible tokens of her being the spirit of my daughter as gave me no less satisfaction than admiration and delight."

Sometime later, the ghost of Nelly Butler materialized, floating over a field, and frightened Captain Blasdell's son, Paul, to such an extent that he ran home. That night, Nelly's voice rose up from the cellar, scolding Paul for not giving her a proper greeting.

By May 1800, Nelly's ghost materialized, wearing "a shining white garment" before twenty people gathered in the Blasdell's cellar. According to one witness, "At first the apparition was a mere mass of light, then it grew into a personal form, about as tall as myself ... the glow of the apparition had a constant, tremulous motion. At last the personal form became shapeless, expanded every way and then vanished in a moment." Some described her as having "a shining halo around her head." Her voice was "shrill but mild and pleasant."

On another occasion, Nelly appeared before two hundred people, giving her usual sermons and making predictions. She prophesied the deaths of Captain Blasdell's wife and his father as well as the future marriage of Lydia to her widowed husband, George Butler. When Captain Blasdell asked Nelly why she didn't appear in the house, she told him, "I do not wish to frighten the children."

Reverend Abraham Cummings became alarmed that people were taking Nelly so seriously, especially when it came to her sermons. He didn't believe in ghosts himself and worried about those who did. He'd heard people repeating things Nelly said such as: "Although my body is consumed and turned to dust, my soul is as much alive as before I left my body."

Unconvinced, Rev. Cummings hastened to the Butler home, intent on exposing the ghost as some form of trickery, but something stopped him—and that something was Nelly Hooper Butler.

William Oliver Stevens describes their strange encounter in his 1945 book *Unbidden Guests: A Book of Real Ghosts*. According to Stevens, white rocks floated up from the ground, joined together and took the shape of a rose-tinged orb. It suddenly flashed and took the form of a child-sized woman. When he spoke to it, "the figure expanded to normal size." She was "glorious with rays of light shining from her head all about and reaching to the ground."

This was enough to make him a believer. Rev. Cummings wrote *Immortality Proved by the Testimony of Science*, which was published in 1859.

Eventually Lydia Blasdell married George Butler, but she also died ... in childbirth, just as Nelly had before her. After Lydia's death, Nelly vanished, and George Butler, in great remorse, never married again.

(72) Lubec

Passamaquoddy Bay

When the shores of Lubec are blanketed in pea soup fog, the ghost of a beautiful Passamaquoddy maiden is said to walk along the beaches. Locals call her 'the Walking Woman,' as seen by Captain Ed Cook

The Walking Woman floats along these shores near Lubec. *Courtesy of Bob Gray.*

and his crew. Clad in white with her long hair streaming behind her, she glides about two feet off the ground and easily keeps pace with boats. No one knows who the Walking Woman is or why she haunts the waters of Passamaquoddy Bay. Appearing between Lubec and Calais over the years, she has been seen by many.

The Lubec Light
74 Washington Street

This building is home to Lubec's newspaper, *The Lubec Light*, and is said to be haunted by the ghost of a lady whom locals believe may be either Mrs. Bradley or Mrs. Kelly. She's not the frightening type, but since she startled a local repairman, he refuses to go into this newspaper building alone. Since other businesses also occupy the building, chances are this spirited missus is seldom lonely.

A ghost lady is believed to haunt this office building in Lubec.
Courtesy of Bob Gray.

Aroostook County

Haynesville Woods, South Oakfield Road Cemetery, Industrial Park, St. Froid Lake, Violette Settlement

(73) Haynesville Woods,
Route 2A from Macwahoc to Houlton

The forty-mile stretch of Route 2A from Haynesville to Houlton has long been known as 'Haynesville Woods Road.' Truckers use this route for hauling loads of potatoes and lumber between Maine and Canada. The 1965 Allagash Records hit, "A Tombstone Every Mile" (written by Daniel Fulkerson/sung by Dick Curlass) immortalized Haynesville Woods as one of the nation's most dangerous highways. Part of the chorus mentions that there would be a tombstone every mile for every trucker "lost in them woods," and implies that going to hell couldn't be half as bad as driving "that river of ice" in the winter.

The song makes no mention of the ghost of Haynesville Woods—a young woman who began hitchhiking here after her car broke down. It was night and raining hard. Apparently, she saw a big truck coming along and stuck out her thumb, but the driver didn't see her … She was killed instantly.

On rainy nights, the White Lady of Haynesville Woods stands beside the road, trying to thumb a ride. According to drivers who've seen her, she's quite pale and shaken—and after they pick her up she vanishes without a word.

Another Haynesville legend concerns the thin spots found occasionally along the road. These thin spots are believed to account for some of the lost truckers' stories over the years, places where the road is so dark that light cannot penetrate—and all matter, including drivers and their vehicles, become swallowed up by these 'dimensional gateways' best described in the writings of H.P. Lovecraft. A word to the wise: if your headlights suddenly seem to go out, don't keep on truckin'.

(74) South Oakfield Road Cemetery, Linneus

There is a very small, old cemetery on this road (with a larger, newer cemetery behind it) and locals claim passing cars have a tendency to stall near this graveyard. Some claim to have heard cries and screams coming from the graves. In 1999, someone put an old rocking chair in front of the cemetery. After watching it 'rock' as if someone were sitting in it, several people went to great lengths to remove the rocker — taking it to another town and throwing it from a bridge, but it always returned within days to the same spot.

(75) Industrial Park, Houlton

During World War II, there was a German POW camp at the Army air base in Houlton. (It was one of seven in the state.) In May 1946, Camp Houlton was shut down. Little remains of the camp today except the cement foundations of the buildings and a WWII airport control tower. Some folks living nearby were so poor they drank Sterno and one night a bunch of them overdosed. Their raucous spirits are said to haunt the area around Paddy Holler and Industrial Park.

(76) St. Froid Lake, Quimby, Winterville Plantation

During hunting season in 1926, four deer hunters traipsed into the woods in Quimby one morning. Hoping for a good day of hunting, the men went off by themselves, agreeing to meet back at their campsite at St. Froid Lake by nightfall.

Three of the hunters showed up at the campsite, but the hunter named Allen never arrived. The trio called his name and searched the ever-darkening woods near the lake. They agreed it was pointless to search for him in the dark, so they waited until daybreak.

After a few hours of searching, they decided to go to Eagle Lake for help. Every able-bodied person lent a hand in the search for Allen. Autumn nights in Maine can be quite chilly, and no one could guess what had happened to the lost hunter. Had he fallen down and been knocked unconscious? Was he attacked by a black bear? Had he been killed by accident by another hunter? Had his gun misfired, exploding in his face? A long line of volunteers combed through the woods unsuccessfully for three days.

The following year, a different group of hunters camping at St. Froid Lake heard a man in the distance calling for help. Every one of them recognized Allen's voice at once. They picked up their lanterns and searched the woods, yelling for Allen, walking in the direction of his voice.

Then the wind stopped blowing and Allen's pleas for help grew silent. Over the years, many an outdoorsman has heard the voice of the lost hunter calling for help.

(77) Violette Settlement, Fort Kent

Violette is almost as far north as you can get in Maine. Located in the town of Fort Kent on Settlement Road just off St. John Road (Route 161 West), the village was named after the numerous Violette families who settled the area. It is said to be one of the most haunted villages in Maine. The natives who live there are of Acadian French and Maliseet Indian descent.

The haunting that continues to this day started back in the 1950s on a family farm. The head of the family was a scourge of a man who abused his family and their animals. (Some believe he murdered his wife and daughters as no traces of them were ever found.) When his eldest son turned sixteen the father forced him to quit school even though he had done extremely well in his studies. He was then expected to work from sunrise until long after sundown on the family farm.

Not long afterward, the boy died from hunger and abuse. Then his father died in his barn, which eventually burned to the ground.

The boy's ghost is said to haunt the third floor of Violette Settlement School, and even in death, he hides from his father, whose ghost haunts the school grounds but doesn't come inside. In the 1970s, children complained of an unseen "bad man" who scratched and bruised them until he was driven off by an exorcism conducted by the village priest.

A decade later, numerous people described a two-legged beast wearing some sort of heavy cloak that roamed the settlement at night. If encountered inside one's home, the priest has instructed people to open their windows and doors and sweep the apparition outside with a broom.

Penobscot County

(78) Devil's Gulch, Owlsboro Road, Mt. Chase, Patten

Less than five miles north of Patten center, on Owlsbury Road toward Mt. Chase, drivers should slow down by the ravine known as Devil's Gulch; it's where a woman and her newborn baby lost their lives in the early 1900s. According to stories about the tragic accident, she lost control one evening when a carriage wheel sunk into the soft shoulder of the road. The wagon rolled over several times, crashing at the bottom of the gulch, and wasn't discovered until the next day. Some say the woman's baby was never found.

Locals claim the woman's ghost wanders Owlsbury Road, holding a lantern, desperately searching. Some report that if you stop and ask the woman what she's looking for, she sadly replies, "My baby." Some have heard the piercing wails of a human infant coming from the gulch over the years, but searches always turn up nothing.

(79) Brownville Road
Route 11, Millinocket

Maine has its share of road ghosts and Millinocket's White Lady is no exception. Since the 1940s, she has been sighted walking along Brownville Road (Route 11) near Green Bridge on fog-laden nights.

According to local lore, a young couple crashed their car into a ditch on their way home to Millinocket from their honeymoon. Unable to get the car back onto the road, the husband told his bride to stay by the car while he walked to town for help. He wasn't gone long, but when he returned, his bride was gone, never to be seen alive again. Her body was never found, however some say their rusting car still lies upside down in a ditch to this day. Had the bride been disoriented in the accident and tried to follow her husband in the dark? Did she stumble into one of the many lakes along the road and drown? Was she carried off and killed by a bear? Did she get lost and die of exposure? No one will ever know.

Those who've stopped to help the young woman claim she's looking for a ride into town, but she always vanishes before she gets there.

(80) Orono

Hauck Auditorium
University of Maine

Hauck Auditorium was designed by architect A.J. Harriman. It was dedicated on October 18, 1963 and named in honor of Dr. Arthur A. Hauck who had served as the president of the University of Maine. In 2003, members of the Maine Paranormal Research Association teamed up with four student skeptics to investigate hauntings at UMO.

While they found several dorms and a frat house to be haunted, they didn't find any convincing activity in the lobby of Hauck Auditorium. They weren't permitted inside to investigate and concluded that if the auditorium was haunted, it was probably due to residual energy.

Many believe Hauck Auditorium is haunted. Some claim it's visited occasionally by former drama students, directors, and Dr.

Hauck himself. In the 1990s, lighting technicians were perplexed by an extra dancer on the set of Guys and Dolls. Every time they moved the lights toward the mysterious performer, the person moved into the shadows. Irritated by the "wise-guy" on stage, they took a head count at the end of the performance. No one else, not even the performers, noticed any extra actors in their midst.

(81) Bangor

Bangor Historical Society,
Thomas A. Hill House,
159 Union Street

Bangor was the world's busiest lumber port in the late 1800s to early 1900s. During this time, a man named Samuel Dale served as mayor of Bangor. Records show he'd been elected twice. On December 24, 1871, his wife and two foster children returned home from church to find him dead. (By some accounts his corpse was found in the bathroom; others say he died in the bedroom.) Many believe he committed suicide.

In 1871, Mayor Dale began a fundraising campaign to help the city of Chicago recover from the Great Fire. Bangor residents had a lot of empathy for Chicago; decades earlier they'd suffered a terrible fire themselves. The fundraising was doing well until nearly $10,000 went missing and the finger-pointing began. Most people accused Mayor Dale of stealing the money to fund a lavish party for President Ulysses Grant. According to accounts, the party was a grand affair. Lavish gifts were bestowed to guests including Bangor's wealthiest people, the lumber and shipping barons. In midst of the festivities, Mayor Dale realized that the invitation for the guest of honor, President Grant, had not been delivered. He left the party and hurried to The Bangor House to invite the President in person.

Bangor Mayor Samuel Dale continues to haunt the Thomas A. Hill House.

Thus President Grant attended the mayor's party, but he didn't stay long. Even so, everyone considered the party a "rousing success." More funds were donated for the Chicago fire benefit, but the next day, the money was gone. As months passed, people surmised Mayor Dale had taken the funds—not only to fund the party but to renovate parts of his residence as well.

He would have gone to Christmas Eve services with his family, but stayed home due to a stomachache. After his death, his stomach was sent to Boston for analysis. The outcome was never made public, but most figured the cause of death was self-induced poisoning.

Mayor Dale's home was originally the Thomas A. Hill House, designed by Richard Upjohn in Greek Revival style and built around

1835. It is now the headquarters for the Bangor Historical Society and over the years they've witnessed such events as lights turning on and off for no apparent reason, doors that swing open and shut on their own, an office computer that logs onto the Internet by itself and eerie, unexplainable sounds throughout the house. Many believe, including office workers for the Historical Society, that Mayor Dale never actually left the building. His ghost is not frightening; he's considered a prankster and it appears he enjoys playing tricks on the staff by moving paperwork from one spot to another.

The Bangor Historical Society provides maps for self-guided walking tours through eight of the city's historical districts.

The next haunted house is located across the street from the historical society. The Isaac Farrar Mansion is at 166 Union Street. Designed by Richard Upjohn in 1833, the mansion was built around 1845 and presented as a wedding gift from Isaac Farrar to his wife. It's a work of Greek Revival style coupled with English regency and graced with beautiful carved Santo Domingo mahogany paneling, bookcase doors, marble fireplaces and stained glass windows. The mansion is believed to be haunted by the ghost of a distraught governess. This mansion is open to the public for a $1 admission fee.

The ghost of a distraught governess haunts the Isaac Farrar Mansion in Bangor.

Al Brady's Grave
Mount Hope Cemetery
1048 State Street

Bangor's Mount Hope is a garden cemetery, the second of its kind in the United States. It was established as a cemetery in 1834 and was consecrated two years later. Even if you've never visited Bangor, you might have caught a glimpse of Mount Hope Cemetery on film or television. It was the burial/disinterment site for Gage Creed in Stephen King's *Pet Sematary*. It was also a feature of The History Channel's series *Haunted History: Haunted Maine*.

Mount Hope is the final resting place for Al Brady, one of America's most notorious gangsters, a member of the new Dillinger gang, who was slain in a shootout on Bangor's Central Street on Columbus Day, October 12, 1937. Brady, along with Clarence Lee Shaffer, Jr. and Rhuel James Dalhover, formed the New Dillinger Gang. Wanted by the FBI since 1935 for a long string of robberies and the murders of a police officer, an Indiana State Trooper and a store clerk, they'd come to Bangor to purchase guns. What they wanted most was a rapid-fire Thompson sub-machine gun, but playing it cool, they settled for a rifle at Dakin's Sporting Goods Company. They told clerk, Louis Clark, they were hunters.

Clark obviously didn't believe them. He waited until they left, then notified his boss, Everett "Shep" Hurd, who relayed the information to Bangor Police Chief Thomas Crowley.

Policeman Crowley doubted they were members of the New Dillinger Gang. To his knowledge, these strangers hadn't broken any laws, but the following day, C.E. Silsbury, a clerk at the sporting goods store Rice and Miller, reported the suspicious purchase of three 32-calibur pistols. Crowley knew something was up; these men likely weren't hunters as they'd claimed. He contacted the FBI.

Mount Hope Cemetery.

Four days after the purchase of the pistols at Rice and Miller, they visited Dakin's again, buying another rifle, and asking Everett Hurd if he stocked any Tommy guns. He told them a Thompson rapid-fire sub-machine gun would have to be special ordered. The order was then filled out, all the while Hurd knew his clerk's suspicions were correct; who would go deer hunting with a Tommy gun? Besides that, Tommy guns were illegal.

On October 9, 1937 one of the three gangsters stopped at Dakin's and asked if their Tommy gun had arrived. It hadn't. Hurd told them to check again later. That day, fifteen FBI agents with fifteen Indiana and Maine State Troopers got into position at Market Square.

October 12 was a gorgeous, sunny morning. Around 8:30 a.m., the gangsters parked their Buick on Central Street. Brady waited in the backseat, keeping lookout, as Shaffer went into the store. Dalhover watched for police near the storefront. None of them suspected there were two FBI agents waiting for them inside. Casually, Shaffer walked over to the counter and said, "Now about that stuff I ordered..." and that's when Agent Walter Walsh, an FBI sharpshooter, stuck a gun in his ribs from behind and ordered him to surrender. The two men wrestled and Shaffer was knocked to the floor. Agent Walsh saw Dalhover fire two shots from outside the store, breaking the storefront window. As he went after Dalhover, Agent Walsh was hit in the shoulder.

A hail of bullets rained down from FBI agents across the street and along the rooftops. Shaffer fell. Agents rushed to the car and ordered Brady out. As he slid across the backseat, he reached for his gun, and climbing out of the car, he fired. The FBI gunned him down; he ran fifteen or twenty feet and collapsed. The gunfight was over in less than five minutes. Shaffer and Brady were peppered with more than sixty bullets. There was so much blood the fire department arrived to wash the street. According to the feature article in the *Bangor Daily News*, "The man who was to make Dillinger look like a piker had met Dillinger's end. He lay grotesquely on his back—a human sieve, his flesh torn into shreds."

A plaque on the sidewalk at 21 Central Street marks the exact spot where Brady died.

Dalhover was apprehended and later executed. Shaffer's body was claimed; Brady's was not. At age twenty-six, Alfred James Brady was buried in an unmarked grave in Mt. Hope Cemetery's Public Grounds, Lot 2119 on October 15, 1937.

Gangster Al Brady died here in a hail of bullets.

Since his death, Brady's ghost has been seen walking through this remote corner of the cemetery as well as along the sidewalk of Central Street where he was killed. Several years ago, some children tried to put markers fashioned from sticks on Brady's grave but every time they did, by the next morning, the marker was gone. No one knows who kept taking them, but many suspect it may have

been the ghost of Al Brady. This final mystery is the kind of thing a gangster like Brady probably would have enjoyed. The rat-a-tat sounds of machine gunfire can still be heard on Central Street on the date of his death.

Brady's gravesite can be found near the end of a dirt road directly across Mt. Hope Avenue from the Korean War Memorial in Mt. Hope Cemetery. Brady's grave is in the next to last lot before the fence. A ground-level headstone was placed upon Brady's grave in September 2007.

Gangster Al Brady's gravesite at Bangor's Mount Hope Cemetery.

Bangor Public Library
145 Harlow Street
(Tarrantine Club)

While at Mt. Hope Cemetery, walk over to the Riverlawn Section of the Corporate Grounds and you'll find the grave of Hannibal Hamlin, Vice-President to Abraham Lincoln. (See the West Paris section for early information.) After the Civil War, Hamlin created the Tarratine Club in Bangor (incorporated May 18, 1900) and served as its president until his death on July 4, 1891.

Research brought me to an entry in an Internet blog describing how on August 2, 1923, Hamlin was removed from his grave and his corpse was taken to an old Indian Burial Ground where it was reinterred, just like in Stephen King's Pet Sematary.

Trust me, Hannibal Hamlin rests in peace at Mt. Hope. Well, maybe not all the time. Some people have claimed to see his ghost sitting on the couch where he died while playing cards at the Tarratine Club. That couch can be found on the second floor of the Bangor Public Library. Over the years, there have been whispers of cold spots and mysterious indentations forming and then vanishing on that piece of furniture.

Thomas Hill Standpipe
Thomas Hill Road

The Thomas Hill Standpipe was built for the city of Bangor in 1897. A.B. Tower designed its architecture and the New Jersey Steel and Iron Company did the construction of the tank. The land it sits on was owned by James M. and Charles Thomas of Bangor. James built the first Bangor Auditorium. With twenty-two men and a portable sawmill, the wooden shell of the standpipe was finished in six months. The standpipe lights are called the "jewels" in the Queen City's crown.

Many believe the standpipe may have been inspiration for the monster's dwelling place in Stephen King's novel IT. Some will tell you the standpipe is haunted—not by a monster, but possibly the ghost of child.

The standpipe holds 1.75 million gallons of water. It's an iron tank with a wooden jacket, standing fifty-feet high. It helps regulate downtown Bangor's water pressure and is registered as a National Historic Landmark. Since an accident in 1940, it was closed to the public, but is opened occasionally every year so folks can climb the staircase to the top. The view from the top of the 110-foot tall shell is magnificent—on a clear day, Mt. Katahdin can be seen in the distance to the north, Camden Hills to the southeast, and the White Mountains to the west.

In 1940, 12-year-old Howard Goodell fell from the railing of the interior stairwell and died the next day. Since then, some claim to have heard a child's voice accompanied by footsteps on the stairs inside the standpipe when no one else is there.

Bangor's crown jewel, the Thomas Hill Standpipe.

The standpipe is open to the public on several days in March, May, July and October. For more information call the Bangor Water District at 207-947-4516.

(82) St. Patrick's Episcopal Church grounds
21 Holyoke Street, Brewer

Brewer is just across the Penobscot River from Bangor. One of America's first Boy Scout troops was founded here in 1909. In 1926, Father Thomas H. Moriarty established Brewer's first St. Joseph's Roman Catholic Church. He lived in the rectory across the street and was described as "riveting," a staunch defender of the faith who dared to stand up in opposition to the KKK. Parishioners knew him to have a "dry Irish wit," and he was a powerful speaker. There have been changes since his death in 1969. His church was torn down and replaced by an Episcopalian church in 1973; his rectory home was eventually made into a bed-and-breakfast inn.

Just after his death and two days before he was buried, Father Moriarty's familiar footsteps were heard pacing as he had done when saying his breviary. Lights turned on and off, drawers opened and closed, and the sounds of his footsteps continued … even after the old rectory was purchased by a doctor when a new rectory was built in 1976.

According to Thomas A. Verde in *Maine Ghosts and Legends*, a woman was approached by a priest while outside her home. She and her family had just moved to Brewer, and it was kind of him to welcome them to the neighborhood. He asked why he hadn't seen her in church and made her promise to bring her family there next Sunday. The priest's name was Father Moriarty.

To find Holyoke Street, turn right from Route 1A (heading northwest) onto North Main Street. The next street on the right from North Main is Holyoke Street.

Piscataquis County

(83) Dover-Foxcroft

Thursday morning, July 24, 1942, a B-17 was seen by at least a dozen people in the Dexter/Dover-Foxcroft area, according to a June 2000 article in the Dirigo Flyer. The bomber was flying low, just over the treetops, and appeared to be in distress due to the sputtering sounds of its engines. Most of the eyewitnesses saw the plane disappear between two ridges and heard its engines stop. It never emerged from the other side of the ridges. One person claimed to have seen it crash into a wooded ridge not far from the highway, but mysteriously, there was no smoke or fire.

State Police and local lawmen, along with searchers from Dow Air Force Base, combed the area but were unable to find any signs of a crashed plane. The search was called off when they learned no bombers were reported missing.

Later that evening, when a reporter from the *Bangor Daily News* phoned in the story of the crash scare to his boss, his call was interrupted several times by a witness who was adamant the plane had actually crashed.

(84) Greenville Inn
East Cove, Greenville

Located in Greenville at the southern tip of Moosehead Lake, construction of the Greenville Inn started in 1885 by lumber baron

William Shaw, and was completed ten years later with carved embellishments and paneling throughout. The Craft family purchased the home in the early 1920s and lived there until the Whiten family of Rockwood bought the house in 1946. They converted it from a family dwelling to an inn. It had a succession of owners until the Johannemann family purchased it in 2003.

The Johannemanns feel that the Greenville Inn is on loan to them and they enjoy sharing its elegance and history with their guests.

They may also share a story or two about their resident ghost. Recently, a guest staying in the older Carriage House suite reported seeing the ghost of a beautiful young lady. She'd just opened her door when the ghost walked by. She could feel the cool breeze as she passed as well as hear the swishing sounds of her old-fashioned, crinoline skirt. This ghost wasn't at all frightening; she may have been the daughter or wife of one of the earlier owners.

Somerset County

(85) Jackman

According to the storyteller Arial, in November 1960, a young hunter named Jim Wheaton was deer hunting in the Belgrade Lakes region when, about an hour before sunset, he fell and broke his knee.

Jim hadn't told anyone where he was going and he was about a half mile from the road. If he was going to get out of the woods alive, he knew he had to crawl, dragging his injured leg through an ice-cold brook. Struggling up an embankment, he slid down several times, then fired three shots from his rifle, hoping someone would hear him and come to his aid.

Moments later, he heard a crashing noise through the underbrush and a big man carrying an old-fashioned lantern appeared. He wore green wool pants and a red warden's jacket. Quickly, he fashioned a splint of branches for Jim's leg and hoisted him onto his shoulder to carry him out of the woods to safety. An ambulance from Oakland took Jim to the hospital.

In January 1976, Martha and Scott Holt came up from Boston for a week of snowmobiling in Jackman. The trails were well marked and went as far as Canada. Just hours before a blizzard was due, Scott and Martha took one last ride around Big Wood Pond. They lost the trail, ran out of fuel, and realized they weren't on Big Wood Pond. It began to get dark and the wind began to blow. They hadn't brought extra fuel, food, water, map or a compass—and they had no idea where they were.

They were almost panicked for they could easily die in the storm, but then they saw a light moving about a half mile away. They yelled and waved and the light came closer. It was a big man carrying an old lantern. He led them to a camp and gave them some coffee to warm them up. When the storm was over, Scott thanked the rescuer and tried to pay him, but he wouldn't hear of it. "Pay me back by helping someone else out someday," he said.

The next day, Scott and Martha tried to find the camp where they'd warmed up and drank coffee. They wanted to thank their rescuer one more time, but the camp was not to be found, even with the help of an experienced guide who knew the area well.

Over a dozen people like Jim, Scott and Martha have been helped or had their lives saved by a big, gentle soul in the Jackman area. He is always described as carrying an old-fashioned lamp, wearing green wool pants and a red warden's jacket. To date, no one has been able to positively identify the good Samaritan of the Jackman Woods.

(86) Flagstaff
Route 27 (between Stratton and Eustis)

In 1949 Flagstaff, Maine became a ghost town when it was flooded to form a 26-mile body of water called Flagstaff Lake. Central Maine Power (CMP) built a dam on Dead River to be used as a reservoir for hydroelectric power. The towns of nearby Dead River and Bigelow were also flooded. Dead River is under the southeast corner, Bigelow is under the south corner (just west of Dead River), and Flagstaff lies beneath the northern part of the lake.

Flagstaff got its name when Benedict Arnold's army stopped here on their way to Quebec and one of his soldiers raised a flag on a pole. The nearby town of Bigelow was named after Captain Timothy Bigelow of Arnold's army who climbed a hill (aptly named

Mount Bigelow) to see if he could spot Quebec. Native Americans called this area Tiaouiadicht.

Through the years, Flagstaff flourished as a farming town with a population of roughly eighty-five people. Between 1893 and 1947, there were over seventy marriages in Flagstaff. In 1924 the Maine legislature granted the rights to Flagstaff to CMP through eminent domain. This action worried everyone in town because it meant that something was probably going to happen to Flagstaff—and it did.

Even before the Long Falls hydroelectric dam was built, water had started pooling up through Flagstaff's main road. People began moving out, taking their cemeteries and church to higher ground. On Halloween 1949, the Flagstaff Post Office closed. By December, no one would stay the winter in Flagstaff. Houses and farms were burnt down; forests were cleared to make ready for the flood. Some people had a very hard time leaving—waiting until the very last moments until they had no choice—and according to the legend about Flagstaff, one man stayed behind. The 77-year-old Captain Wing had always claimed he'd build an ark before leaving his home. He made no plans whatsoever to relocate, and according to former Flagstaffers, he was the final resident remaining in town. He's still there, some claim, for his ghost haunts the lake.

Flagstaff Lake is open to canoeists. Care must be taken because there are places in the lake where the water is very shallow. Stonewalls, cellar holes, fence poles and rusty barbed wire are still present here. Over the years, people have found copper pans, horseshoes, tools, dishes and much more. Relic seekers must have permission from the Maine Forest Service's Department of Conservation before taking any artifacts or items from this area. See www.maine.gov for contact information. The Dead River Area Historical Society at the junction of Routes 16 and 27 has a display of artifacts gleaned from Flagstaff's depths.

(87) Strand Cinema
15 Court Street, Skowhegan

Even if you've never visited Skowhegan, Maine, you may have seen the Strand Cinema in HBO's 2005 movie, *Empire Falls*.

Opening in December 1929, the Strand in Skowhegan was owned and operated by the Dondis family, who owned theaters in Rockland and Calais. Strange occurrences during the upstairs renovations in 1972 led owners Robert and Joanne Perry to believe their theater might very well be haunted. Such occurrences included them getting shocked from wiring when the electricity was off, flying tools and masking tape, and wood stain mysteriously splattering a wall (the can was still on the step ladder, as if untouched).

During the showing of one of the Halloween movies, plaster fell from a balcony, harming no one but startling a group of rowdy kids into silence. In a back room, firewood was restacked in a very peculiar way—and no one but the owner had been back there. Some moviegoers have seen strange handprints suddenly appearing on the movie screen. A trio of Skowhegan youngsters reported sitting in the far left corner of the theater watching a comedy and suddenly becoming so chilled that two of them had to put on jackets. Although no one was seated behind them, they felt fingers jab them on their shoulders, backs and necks. Apparently the jabbing stopped when they got up and changed seats.

The Skowhegan Cinema is regarded at Shadowlands, a paranormal website, as one of the fifty most haunted sites in the U.S.

Leslie Bugbee, a psychic from nearby Cornville, investigated the Strand and reported strange tapping noises, EVPs captured on tape. The source of the noises could not be found. A *Yankee Magazine* photographer accompanying Leslie could not take pictures inside the theater. Outside, his camera worked just fine. He returned inside and the camera failed to work again.

Today, the restored and expanded cinema is under different ownership. No paranormal activity has been reported by the new owner.

Some count Skowhegan's Strand Cinema among America's
top fifty most haunted places.

Kenneber County

(88) Clinton

At the airport, Central Maine Regional of Norridgewock, on June 10, 1962, David Collins and his wife Lizzie, took off in their Cessna 172, headed for Portland. It was just after 11 a.m. and they had unlimited visibility, except for some fat, puffy clouds, the kind that accompany good weather.

Just then, out from behind a cloud, an old-fashioned biplane came flying right at them. David banked hard to the left but he wasn't quite fast enough. The planes clipped each other's wingtips. David and Lizzie turned to see the biplane descend with its torn canvas wing, and David radioed a mayday call on the emergency channel.

Portland, who responded, cleared him for landing, where field agents from the Federal Aviation Administration office awaited his arrival. The Collins couple answered questions and filled out forms, but they were told they couldn't take their plane home until the pilot of the biplane reported the accident.

A week went by. David called the FAA to find out if the other pilot had filed a report. He hadn't. The insurance company thought the accident was a fraud. Weeks turned into months. The insurance company refused to pay to fix the wing and the FAA refused to release the plane.

Nearly a year passed before the FAA and the insurance company reluctantly agreed to take paint samples from the damaged wing. The samples were taken to the FAA Lab in Wichita, Kansas, and a few months after, the results were in. The samples contained yellow paint and cloth fabric that dated back to 1920. With this information, as strange as it sounded, the FAA and the insurance company finally released and repaired David's airplane.

Moving forward to May 1982. Paul Smith, a University of Maine college student, headed from Clinton, Maine for Nebraska to work on a dairy farm belonging to his roommate Todd's parents. One of their first jobs was to clean out an old barn.

The barn was huge; it was four stories tall, and although it was old, it was in excellent condition. It was filled with old farming equipment and junk to almost the second story level. All the old equipment had to be pulled out by tractor and it took the boys almost two weeks of steady work just to get to the hay pile at the back of the barn.

Under the hay, they found an old, yellow biplane, a 1915 Faulkner. It looked to be in great condition, except for some damage to the right wingtip. In the cockpit, they found the pilot's log. The pilot's name was Waldo Peddit and he'd purchased the plane in 1920 in Omaha. From there, he recorded all his flights in detail. The last page was dated Sunday, June 10, 1932. Waldo and his wife, Betsy, left the Omaha Airport to head home. According to the log, they were flying at 3,000 feet when they spotted another plane flying straight at them. Their wing tips collided with what the pilot described as a "bang!" Then they watched the other plane disappear into the sky above them. When they arrived home, the Peddits put their airplane in the barn because there wouldn't be time to fix it until the crops were in. The story fascinated the boys … and it was about to get even better.

That night, Paul Smith's dad called from Maine and Paul told him about the biplane they'd found in the old barn. The story made him shiver—he told Paul he knew a couple from Norridgewalk—twenty years ago, they had a midair collision with a mysterious old biplane.

After Paul's father called him, David Collins wondered if the FAA had ever received a report or heard anything new about the crash. He called a field agent and told him about the biplane the boys had found in Nebraska. The FAA dispatched a field agent to Nebraska to take paint samples from the damaged wing of the biplane.

The paint matched that of David's Cessna, and the paint samples taken from the Cessna matched that of the biplane. The FAA also said there was no way the biplane had been flown within the last fifty years ... but they were able to confirm a letter sent to Omaha Airport dated June 12, 1932 from Waldo Peddit. He'd reported a midair collision with a "strange-looking monoplane."

(89) Maine State House, Augusta

When the State House is empty, it's so quiet one could hear the drop of a pin. However, that's not what a custodian heard one Wednesday morning when she was there alone, dusting. She thought someone was playing a joke on her when she heard someone call out, "Hello!" The voice was that of a woman. The custodian called out, asking who was there and she looked around, but found no one.

A female ghost haunts the Maine State House.

Five minutes later, the light went out in the office she'd been working in. She walked out of the room and found all the other lights were on. When she went back into the office, the light came on again. There was nothing wrong with the bulb or the switch, and this had never happened before.

The custodian described another time when her boss went into the ladies' room to find the sink faucet running. No one else was in there—and strangely, no one could shut the faucet off.

Moments later, the water shut off by itself and the faucet worked normally. All of this was enough to convince the custodian that the State House is haunted by the ghost of a woman.

(90) Hallowell

The brutal 1974 murders of the DeFeo family in Amityville, New York may be the most famous case in which members of the same household were systematically slain in cold blood by a close relative. One hundred sixty-eight years earlier, a Maine family lost their lives in similar fashion: sleeping peacefully until the screaming began … they were killed in their beds,.

On Wednesday, July 9, 1806, 17-year-old James Purrington, Jr. awoke to the sounds of his mother's piercing cries. He leapt from his bed and ran to his bedroom door where he was met by his father brandishing a bloody axe. He turned to run, but Captain James Purrington swung the axe and struck him squarely in the back. When a younger brother awoke and tried to fend off their murderous father, Captain Purrington turned on the younger boy, giving James a chance to escape and run to their neighbors for help.

Augusta was a settlement comprised of mostly English farmers by the turn of the nineteenth century, and neighbors knew and helped one another with the raising of animals and children, care of the sick, sowing and harvesting crops. Not one of them could have ever imagined or predicted the horrific nightmare that became a deadly reality for most of the Purrington family that terrible Wednesday night.

The Purrington family massacre occurred in Hallowell in 1806.

Diarist and midwife Martha Moore Ballad wrote about the Purrington family in her journal. In 1803, she baked bread and pies for them when Betsy Purrington was ill or away. The Purringtons were regular visitors in the Ballard home. Betsy liked to stop by sometimes in the afternoon for tea with Martha. Occasionally, Captain Purrington came by to pick up medicine for his wife or children. Being not only their neighbor and friend, but a nurse as well, meant Martha would be the one to care for the dead. She was 71 years old and did most of the work herself.

In her July 9, 1806 journal entry, Martha wrote that the day had been clear and warm. She and her husband were awakened at three in the morning by neighbors saying Captain Purrington had murdered all his family except James, who was wounded but managed to escape to the home of Dean Wyman. Dean had promptly alerted Jonathan, son of Martha and Ephraim Ballard, that something was terribly wrong at the Purrington house. Martha and her 81-year-old husband arose from their bed and made haste to their neighbors' home where they found the murdered family.

Martha called what she saw there "the most shocking scene that was ever seen in this part of the world." The house seemed bathed in blood. The corpses were carried to the barn where they were carefully washed and "laid out side by side." It was heartbreaking work for Martha; she loved these dear friends. There was 10-year-old Polly Purrington and her older sister with whom Martha had shared her knowledge of herbal remedies, and the baby, Meriah, who was just learning to talk, then 12-year-old Jack and his two little brothers, then their parents. Caring for the corpses took all day; Martha didn't finish until well after sunset. While she was busy with this task, hundreds of people stopped by. Most were curious about the news they'd heard concerning the murders. Some just wanted to look and see what really happened. A few offered to help Martha. "Coffins were brought," writes Ballard, "and the corpses [were] carried in a wagon and deposited in the Augusta Meeting House." Purrington relatives arriving from other towns to attend the funeral stayed with the Ballard family.

The Kennebec Gazette described the gruesome murder-suicide: "In the outer room lay prostrate on his face, and weltering in his gore, the perpetrator of the dreadful deed — his throat cut in the most shocking manner, and the bloody razor lying on the table by his side." Mrs. Betsy Purrington lie in a blood-soaked bed, her head nearly severed from her neck. Beside her, on the floor, lie the body of her 10-year-old daughter who'd no doubt run to her mother upon hearing the frightful cries in the night. In another bedroom, three more daughters lie "dreadfully butchered." The 19-year-old and the 18-month-old were dead. In this room, Martha Purrington alone managed to survive, her body partially covering the baby sister she'd tried to save, despite being "desperately wounded" herself. In another bedroom, the two youngest boys, ages 6 and 8, lie in bed, their throats slashed open. On the hearth, "dreadfully mangled" sprawled the body of the 12-year-old son, his trousers tucked under an arm. He'd been cut down while trying to escape and left a bloody handprint smeared on the breastwork over the fireplace. "The whole house seemed covered with blood," according to the Gazette, "and near the body of the murderer laid the deadly axe."

Captain James Purrington was forty-six years of age. He had recently moved with his wife, Betsy, and their eight children from Bowdoinham to Old Belgrade Road in Augusta (now Hallowell, Maine). By all appearances, the captain was a good man, a yeoman (an old word for independent farmer), who owned a handsome estate. According to 1806 tax records, he was doing quite well for himself and his family: he owned two acres of tilled land, four acres of pasture and ninety-four acres of unimproved land. On the Sunday before the murders, however, Captain Purrington wrote a letter to his brother informing him that he would be dead by the time the letter was delivered. In the letter, he asked that his brother care for his family after he was gone. The strange correspondence was marked with a black death's head sealed with black wax.

Betsy Purrington found her husband's gloomy letter before it was sent and for reasons unknown opened it on Monday, two days before that terrible Wednesday. Reading it gave her great alarm, but the captain assured her that he had no intention whatsoever of committing suicide. He told her he'd experienced a premonition of his own death, nothing more.

Apparently, this was enough to placate Betsy, although she must have known that her husband worried often about his ability to provide for his family and farm. Captain Purrington was a regular churchgoer, a Universalist who believed in equality and in the concept that everyone, regardless of race, creed or religion, would be reconciled with God. On the day of the murders, he did nothing unusual except to sharpen some of his tools, presumably for use the next day. When the family went to bed that night, he stayed up late, reading the bible before reaching for his well-honed axe.

What motivated him to carry out the heinous murders of nearly his entire family? Some of his peers speculated that his Universalist religion, less conservative than that of other churches in the area, may have ultimately led Captain Purrington to murder. Why not kill one's self and family—or anyone else for that matter—if there is no punishment in the hereafter? Perhaps Purrington believed, like John List who killed his own wife and children in 1971, that he was sparing his family from suffering hardship and that they'd all reunite in heaven? This point was heavily argued from the pulpits of area churches; the Methodists, Calvinist Baptists and the Free Will Baptists, yet no one would ever fathom Purrington's motive for murder.

Augusta selectmen carried seven coffins into the South Parish Meeting House on Market Square. The eighth, the Captain's coffin, was left out on the porch. The funeral was somber that dreary day, with no less than three reverends presiding. Afterwards, Betsy Purrington and her children were interred in the northeast corner of Burnt Hill (now part of Mount Vernon Cemetery).

Captain James Purrington, last to be interred, was buried without ceremony under the corner of what is now Winthrop and High streets with his bloody axe and razor thrown into the grave atop his coffin.

Surviving son, James Purrington, attended the family funeral and interment. His sister, Martha, did not. She succumbed to her grievous wounds on July 30.

Charles Elventon Nash in *The History of Augusta* (1904) stated that the locations of the Purrington family graves were lost. However, according to a 2006 article in the *Kennebec Current*, archaeologist Lee Cranmner of the Maine Historic Preservation Commission, working with a crew from Augusta, located the graves in Mount Vernon Cemetery. It is believed Captain Purrington's final resting place remains beneath the street corner of Winthrop and High.

On December 9, 2006, the dedication of a gravestone to mark the Purrington family burial site was held at the City Hall in Augusta.

Hallowell locals claim there is a strange spot near the banks of the Kennebec River on Old Belgrade Road. (Hallowell was once part of the city of Augusta.) This spot is the location where the Purrington house once stood, where seven senseless murders followed by suicide took place. The spot has been seen glowing an eerie green at night and some readers speculate that this may have been the inspiration for Stephen King's 1987 novel The Tommyknockers.

(91) Case Cemetery
Route 17 (Readfield-Manchester town line)

The devil's footprint legend was said to have taken place in the early days of Manchester. Workers were building the road that later became Route 17 when an obstacle halted operations. There was a large rock in their way, one too large and heavy for their teams of oxen to move. After many hours and attempts at prying the rock loose, one man swore that he'd sell his soul to the devil if only the rock would budge. It didn't, and at the end of the day the workers went home.

When they arrived the next morning to resume moving the rock, they were shocked to find the rock was completely moved out of the way, off to the side of the road.

Case Cemetery, probable site of the devil's footprint legend

Even more compelling were the indentations in the rock's surface, which resembled two footprints: one very large, three-toed print, the other a smaller human-shaped footprint, about the size of a man's boot.

The man who had boasted about selling his soul to the devil was nowhere to be found. His ghost is believed to haunt Case Cemetery.

Paranormal investigators Bill and Brenda Washell also deem the cemetery haunted. In a photograph of the Devil's Footprint rock, a weird bright spot showed up on the rock's photo. Members of Maine Paranormal Research Association noticed the temperature dropped to twenty degrees in front of the rock. EVPs recorded a woman moaning, "Get out..." Orbs have been photographed here as well.

According to Bill Washell, when the temperature suddenly drops six or more degrees and the needle of a compass moves twenty-six degrees from true north, spirit activity is nearby.

Some locals tell of the footprint stone being removed about a decade ago … but then, not long after its removal and without plausible explanation for why it was removed and by whom, it reappeared near the cemetery.

(92) Cumston Hall,
95 Main Street, Monmouth
www.cumstonhall.org

Cumston Hall is at the heart of Monmouth. It's home of the Cumston Public Library and The Theater at Monmouth. Henry Cochrane designed the building with music and art in mind; the floor of the auditorium is curved for acoustic resonance—he hired ship carpenters to help in its construction. He also painted murals upon the walls, cherubic frescoes on the ceiling and constructed its many exquisite stained glass windows. For its dedication day, he composed the music and conducted the orchestra. Cumston Hall, complete with indoor plumbing, was the first building in Monmouth to have electric lights.

He decorated his first church in 1887; marbleizing plaster, wood and gold leaf gilding by hand. He painted wall murals and was recognized for his superior craftsmanship and talent. Before his death in 1946, Cochrane had been commissioned to decorate more than four hundred public buildings. Some feel that his most spectacular murals were done in the 1927 decoration of Lewiston's Kora Temple. He wrote the hymn "Prince of Peace," which is still sung in Monmouth churches. His painting, "The Man on Horseback", hangs in Monmouth's Methodist Church. In 1920, he was appointed by Governor Carl E. Milliken to be chairman of the Maine Centennial Committee. He wrote and produced a film, *The Romance of Maine*. In short, Henry Cochrane was a true Renaissance man.

The building was named in honor of Dr. Charles Cumston, headmaster of Boston English High School. After retiring to Monmouth, Dr. Cumston gave the town the grand hall that would house town offices, town meetings, a public library and auditorium. Until 1952, all school functions took place there.

Cumston Hall was named in 1976 to the National Register of Historic Places. Henry Cochrane's ghost has been seen here by many people—it appears he visits to make sure people are still enjoying his fine work. Cumston Hall is also home to the ghost of a janitor hired the first day it opened to the public on June 27, 1900. Some say the poor man hung himself in the basement.

Henry Cochrane's ghost has been known to visit Cumston Hall in Monmouth.

Madame Lillian Nordica has been heard in this Farmington auditorium since her death in 1914.

Franklin County

(93) Nordica Auditorium
2nd floor of Mallet Hall
University of Maine at Farmington

Opera singer Madame Lillian Nordica was born Lillian Bayard Norton in 1857 in Farmington, Maine. She attended the New England Conservatory of Music in Boston and sang in London, Rome and for Tsar Alexander II in St. Petersburg. She was the first American to perform at Germany's Bayreuth Festival. In 1911, she performed in Merrill Hall (later named Nordica Auditorium in her memory).

Madame Nordica died of pneumonia on May 10, 1914 on the island of Java. Her death may have been long ago and far away, but her spirit is believed to haunt Nordica Auditorium, where her portraits grace the walls. Almost every night, close to midnight, it is said her sweet voice can be heard wafting and echoing through the auditorium. She has been heard by students and teachers alike.

Erika Hoddinott, president of UMF's journalism club, told *Maine Today Morning Sentinal* correspondent Rod Labbe, "Nordica's pretty scary, even during daytime. Floorboards creak, lights flicker on and off. Late at night, you detect an odd, disquieting presence. And the singing! Wow."

Oxford County

(94) Bethel

The Moses Mason House Museum
Broad Street

Dr. Moses A. Mason was born in Dublin, New Hampshire in 1789. He was ten years old when his family moved to Bethel, Maine where he worked as a physician's apprentice under Dr. James Ayer of Newfield. He and his wife, Agnes M. Straw Mason, moved into their Bethel home in 1813 where he began a medical practice. In 1815, he became Bethel's first postmaster; the post office was part of his house. He served on the Board of County Commissioners and the Bethel Board of Selectmen, as well as a Justice of the Peace. From 1821 to 1866, he married forty-three couples, and it was his kindness to return his fee to the bride as a wedding gift. In 1833, he was elected as a Jacksonian Democrat for the 2nd District in Maine's House of Representatives. Dr. Mason died in 1866.

Dr. Mason's house is the oldest building in Bethel's National Register Historic District. One of the most interesting aspects of the house is the wall murals of seascapes and landscapes painted by Rufus Porter on both sides of the front hall. Visitors at the Moses Mason House Museum claim to have heard footsteps walking through unoccupied rooms accompanied by unidentified noises and the sounds of people talking.

The Mason House is open to the public year-round (closed on Mondays). It's shown by appointment from November to May. Admission: $3 adults, $1.50 children ages 6-12.

The Bethel Inn Resort™
7 Broad Street

The Bethel Inn was built in 1913 in the elegant style of Colonial Revival, funded by pioneer neurologist Dr. John George Gehring and five of his grateful patients when Bethel's Prospect Hotel burned in 1911. The Inn began as a place for the doctor's patients to stay during their treatments, his specialty being therapy for nervous disorders. Dr. Gehring was born in 1857 in Cleveland, Ohio and moved to Bethel, Maine in 1887. A year later, he married Susie Marian True Farnsworth of Bethel. He died at age seventy-five of a heart attack on September 12, 1932. Robert Herrick's 1908 novel *The Master of the Inn* was based on Dr. Gehring and his Inn. On May 22, 1979, Richard D. Rasor purchased the Inn, and in less than a decade, endorsed the 7.5 million dollar expansion project that turned the Inn into the magnificent resort that it is today.

Throughout the years many people have reported seeing a female ghost wearing old-fashioned clothing strolling down the corridor of the Inn. No one knows who she is, but it is suspected that she may have been one of Dr. Gehring's patients who has returned for a visit.

The ghost of a lady in old-fashioned clothes strolls the corridors of The Bethel Inn Resort.

(95) Snow Falls,
Route 26, West Paris
The Mollyockett Motel faq.website

Molly Ockett, the great Abenaki medicine woman, was born in Fryeburg. Her birth name may have been 'Singing Bird', but she was baptized as Mary Agatha (Molly Ockett is likely the way she pronounced her Christian name) in 1741; she died August 2, 1816, under the open sky as were her wishes. Her gravestone in Andover says she was the last of the Pequakets. Molly used to walk through the woods from Andover to Paris, Maine on what is now known as the Molly Ockett Trail (Route 26), part of the Longfellow Trail from Boston to Canada.

She collected roots and herbs of healing nature and provided remedies for the English settlers in the area, never accepting more than a copper penny in return for her services. For a long time, Molly was the only doctor these people had. Her wisdom of medicine saved the life of a baby in West Paris; his name was Hannibal Hamlin and he became Abraham Lincoln's Vice President. (For the article about Hamlin, see Tarratine Club, Bangor, Maine)

Molly believed the springs in Poland, Maine had remarkable medicinal powers; she used to visit the Wentworth Ricker family at their inn, which eventually became the Poland Springs Resort. She passed on her wisdom to those who would listen, good advice, such as: "Never marry a woman who doesn't love flowers or trust someone who hates music or children. When you find yourself in bad company, leave at once and remember that your worst problems are usually a result of ignorance."

There are many stories about this wise woman, including one about a curse. One winter Molly was walking from Andover to Paris Hill, but the going proved very difficult. During a blizzard, she stopped at Trap Corner (junction of Routes 26 and 219) and buried her satchel beneath a bear trap so that it might be found if she died. She managed to make her way to Snow Falls (now part of West Paris) where she knocked upon a miller's door to ask for directions and shelter. When she was refused both, Molly cursed the mill at Snow Falls. In a few years, it burned down but even today people still believe in the Snow Falls Curse, for businesses near the old mill seem doomed to failure.

Once Snow Falls' busy schoolhouse, The River Restaurant on Route 26 serves up lunches, dinners, and cocktails in its English Style Pub, with a menu including venison and bison dishes. The Mollyockett Motel is just up the road (Route 26) from The River Restaurant. Both businesses have embraced the history of Snow Falls and are doing well, so perhaps Molly Ockett's curse, like that of the Saco River, has finally petered out.

The River Restaurant, one of the few businesses to survive the Snow Falls curse.

In 1994 Marge Bruchac wrote and produced a song titled 'Molly Ockett's Song,' on her Voices in the Woods CD. In nearby Bethel, the third Saturday in July is set aside for a festival honoring Molly Ockett.

(96) Western Maine Sanatorium
Greenwood Mountain Road Loop
West Minot, Hebron

In the early 1900s Western Maine Sanatorium was a place where people suffering with tuberculosis were kept. In those days, relief was provided with plenty of fresh air and sunshine. Postcards dating back to this time show patients relaxing outdoors and playing games.

The Hebron facility opened in 1901, and by 1921, it contained one hundred and nine beds. Back then, according to the Standard Hospital Asylum and Institution Directory, it paid its nurses $6-$10 a week for men and $5-$9 a week for women. The Sanatorium shut down in July 1959.

Near the site of the old buildings, people have reported on occasion hearing the sounds of breaking glass, like that of windows being shattered, but upon inspection, no one can find any broken glass. Are they hearing the former sounds of a football or softball hitting a window that is no longer there? Western Maine Sanatorium was located on Greenwood Mountain Road Loop on what is now Maine Public Reserve Land.

(97) Scribner Hill Cemetery
Scribner Hill Road, Otisfield

Some believe Scribner Hill Cemetery is the actual site of the devil's footprint legend (see Case Cemetery for story).

Old cemeteries, like this one on Scribner Hill, are often haunted.

(98) Peace With-Inn Bed and Breakfast
254 West Fryeburg Road
(Rt. 113N), Fryeburg
www.peacewithinn.com

The Peace With-Inn Bed and Breakfast began as a four-bedroom farmhouse built by Samuel Bradley in 1750. On May 13, 1777, he sold his property to David Hardy, whose descendants lived in the house for ten generations. In 1941, Alice Webster Black and her husband, Chester Black, inherited the farmhouse from her aunt, Mrs. Walter Hardy. They lived there until they died in the mid 1970s, leaving their estate to their daughter, Barbara Black Lawrence and her husband William Lawrence, who occupied the house during vacations. In 1998, the Lawrences sold the home to Marvin and Katheryn Milbury, who turned the farmhouse into a bed and breakfast, the Peace With-Inn. When the Milburys retired in 2002, they sold the Inn to Ashley and Greg Link, who continued operating the bed and breakfast with genuine hospitality reflected in their logo, "Come as guests … leave as friends!"

It is believed the ghosts of Chester Black and his wife Alice visit the home they loved in life. Floorboards creaking with the sounds of footsteps when no one is there, decorations being re-arranged by unseen hands, and doors mysteriously locking are some of the signs of a haunting. The Links don't mind their presence and consider them their "spiritual innkeepers."

(99) Tower Road
Durgintown, Hiram

Partially unpaved, Tower Road connects the towns of Hiram and Cornish. This two-mile stretch of road winds through the woods, hills and a bog, the runoff from Barnes Brook, a Saco River tributary. Locals from Hiram and Cornish claim there's something very weird about the bog, especially after midnight. It might be swamp gas, but that doesn't explain why drivers claim a strange force pushes down on the trunks of their cars or the beds of their pickup trucks as they drive along, accompanied by the uncanny feeling that they're not alone, that something or someone is watching them.

Ghosts Debunked

Hendricks Head Light and Union Cemetery, West Southport (32)

Built in 1829, located on Southport Island at the mouth of the Sheepscot River, Hendricks Head Light stands at forty-three feet above sea level.

According to the story, in March of 1870 lighthouse keeper Jeruel Marr and his wife watched helplessly from the shore as a ship was torn asunder on ledges just off the island. They were desperate to rescue the passengers—they could see them clinging to the rigging; they could hear their screams—but the savage wind and seas dashed all hope of rescue. Debris from the wreck was swept ashore; one item, caught by Marr with his gaff hook, was a box secured between two feather mattresses. The box contained a baby, alive and shivering with cold, with a hastily penned note from her doomed mother. The baby was named Seaborn. Having lost their own daughter, the Marrs raised her as their own. (In some versions, she is adopted by a doctor and his wife.) A ghost thought to be Seaborn's young mother has purportedly been seen walking the beach near the lighthouse in the winter.

Not true! Thanks to research by Barbara Rumsey of the Boothbay Region Historical Society, the story about baby Seaborn is pure fiction, based on a 1900 novel titled *Uncle Terry - A Story of the Maine Coast* by Charles Clark Munn. In his book, Munn describes a lighthouse called 'The Cape.' located on the mainland about five miles south of Hendricks Head. (The Cuckolds Light is the only lighthouse south of Hendricks head, on an island off Southport's southern tip.) According to Munn's story, in 1882 a baby was secured between mattresses and sent ashore during a shipwreck. She was rescued by lighthouse keeper Terry Silas and raised by Uncle Terry and Aunt 'Lissy' Melissa in Southport. Her name was Etelka 'Telly' Peterson, born in Stockholm, Sweden. Eventually, Telly gets rich, finds love and moves away—end of story.

Southport's real ghost, called 'the Lady of the Dusk' by Rose O'Brien in a 1956 article in the *Lewiston Journal*, has been seen by many at nightfall, sometimes under a full moon, sometimes in the pea soup fog, but always dressed in black.

The last time Louise G. Meade was seen alive was in the early December afternoon of 1931, asking directions to Hendricks Head on Southport Island because she wanted "one last good look" before she went out west. Hendricks Head Lighthouse keeper, Charles Knight, thought he caught a glimpse of her just before dark, the flicker of a shadow slipping around the corner of the Connor's summer cottage by a stonewall. He called out to her several times, but received no answer and gave up. After her body washed ashore, the poor lighthouse keeper blamed himself for minding his own business instead of going after her.

Labels on her clothing were the only identifying marks ever found and they were from Lord & Taylor, a fashionable New York City clothing store. For years afterwards, on the anniversary of the stranger's death, a long, black limousine would drive down Hendricks Head Road and park near the location where her body was found. Was she mixed up with rumrunners? Had she gone down to the Head to signal smugglers? Was she killed because she knew too much?

The store owner's wife was closing up the West Southport Post Office end of the store when she saw the lady, who stopped and said, "I'm on my way to the ocean. Which way shall I go?" The stranger said she was looking for a "sweep of the open ocean," and Mrs. Pinkham directed her to Hendricks Head, warning her that it was going to be dark soon. The lady thanked her and left. She described the lady as a refined, quiet woman in her 40s. Not a raving beauty but "nice looking."

The stranger had come by bus to Boothbay Harbor on December 1, 1931, checking in at the Fullerton Hotel, and signing her name as Louise G. Meade. She left a suitcase behind, but there was nothing to identify her save the Lord & Taylor dress and coat she'd been wearing when she washed up on shore. On the day of her death, she'd asked several townspeople where she could get a good view of the deep ocean. In Boothbay, she was told to go down to the town wharf, but that didn't interest her. Someone must have told her about Hendricks Head, for she walked from Boothbay to Southport, and after speaking with Mrs. Pinkham at the post office, to Hendricks Head. A while later, lighthouse keeper Charles Knight came into the store and Mrs. Pinkham asked him if he'd seen the woman walking down to Hendricks Head. He hadn't—he'd just walked up the same road the lady had walked down—they had to have passed one another, but he was quite sure he hadn't seen her. He promised to look out for her.

Retracing his footsteps the next day, it appeared that Knight had walked right past her on the road to Hendricks Head, but no wonder he hadn't seen her—she'd dodged into the woods on the north side of the road near the top of Beach Hill. After he passed, she stepped out of the woods and continued her walk.

The next morning Willis Brewer, a fisherman, went out to look for her. He found her shoe prints and followed them to the beach where she'd stood for a while, and then her footprints led him up the road to Salt Pond (presumably lost in the dark). She then returned to Hendricks Head Road and the Connor's cottage. According to Charlie Pinkham, she must have seen the lights in the lighthouse residence—but she retraced her steps for about one hundred feet, going west down past the Connor's garage. At any rate, she must have heard Charles Knight calling to her. Why didn't she answer him? Why did she walk away?

Her body was found December 6, 1931 with a leather belt fastened tightly around her wrists and run through the handles of a heavy flat iron. The coroner declared her a probable suicide, death by drowning. Detectives from New York City came down, the Missing Persons Bureau was checked and re-checked, but no one could identify her. She was buried January 8, 1932 in the old Union Cemetery in West Southport on the road to Hendricks Head. Fieldstones and a blank headstone mark her grave beneath a large tree and off to one side.

Whoever she was, she won't be forgotten because she keeps coming back.

The lighthouse and its grounds are not open to the public, but can be viewed from the beach along Hendricks Hill Road. Union Cemetery is open to the public.

High Point Cliff
Route 1 (47)

High Point Cliff is said to overlook the ocean just off Route 1 in Belfast; however, I've been unable to locate this particular cliff. Until a historical record of Barbara Houndsworth of Belfast, Maine is found, we should assume this story to be a legend. Additionally, Belfast was incorporated as a town in 1773. Originally part of the Muscongus/Waldo Patent, its first settlers purchased lots in 1769 for 25-cents an acre, over sixty years after the last death sentences for witchcraft were carried out in America.

According to the story, following an outbreak of distemper among dogs and cats and a plague that affected cattle, Barbara Houndsworth was accused of practicing witchcraft when her neighbor fell mysteriously ill. Perhaps she'd tried to save the neighbor with her knowledge of herbs and homemade medicines and failed. According to other variations of this tale, she may have poisoned her husband and/or their child.

The condemned woman was brought to the town square in chains for the reading of her sentence. Someone threw a rock meaning to strike Goodwife Houndsworth, but missed and struck the town clerk in the forehead. In the chaos that ensued, Houndsworth managed to escape and ran into the woods toward the coast. She emerged on the rocky beach to be greeted by a storm of wind and rain. Unable to bear the weather, her pursuers turned back for town. Just after that, Houndsworth slipped and fell from the cliff to the sea where she drowned.

According to the legend, her chain-bound ghost, accompanied by the sound of screams, has been reported running terrified along the eastern shores of Belfast.

Pocock Island (72)

According to a December 19, 1874 article in the *New York Sun*, Pocock Island is located seventeen miles off the Washington County coast. I've lived on the coast of Maine just about all my life, but I have yet to find it so it's probably safe to assume it's as fictional as its ghost story.

According to the Sun article, a businessman's letter had been mailed from Pocock describing how members of the Naugatuck Yacht Club found shelter on the island during an August storm—and that one of the club members was a medium, a man who not only spoke with the dead, but was capable of making them appear to the living.

This accomplished seer led a séance in the schoolhouse on Pocock to entertain his friends and their hosts as they waited out the storm. During the séance, he made ghosts materialize and come out of a wooden cabinet. The first was an Indian Chief named Hockamock. The second ghost was an aunt of one of the yacht club members, and then a small child followed by a Canadian who only spoke French, then Maine's first governor, William King. After the dutiful spirits went back into the cabinet, the lanterns were turned down to dim flickers, and the final ghost emerged—someone recognized by every Pocock resident.

Imagine the shock of the islanders when fisherman John Newbegin stepped out of the cabinet in his heavy boots with a fish in his hand. In April 1870, Newbegin drank himself to death and was buried on the island. With his free hand, he reached over and turned the flame up on a lantern before taking a seat among his shocked friends and neighbors.

The letter went onto describe the Lazarian John Newbegin as "affable and even communicative" as well as "perfectly aware of his doubtful status." Newbegin was thinking of running for the state legislature and proposed that he was "the first of a possible flood" of immigrants from the spirit world.

Shocking, yes! However, not one iota of it was true. The article and the letter were the clever inventions from the mind of a young journalist named Edward P. Mitchell, however he so impressed the editor of the New York Sun that he was offered a staff position with the newspaper.

Striar Textile Mill,
Ayers Island (80)

Ayers Island derived its name from the surname of some of Orono's first settlers as far back as 1774. Ayers Island spans sixty-two acres and has been an industrial site on the Penobscot River in Orono for at least one hundred seventy years, starting with sawmills. Surveys from 1838 show several sawmills on the island and some sort of bridge, perhaps a log boom that connected Ayers Island to the mainland of Orono. By 1886, there were nineteen sawmills on the island, including a machine shop. In 1946 the Striar Company purchased the island and the old pulp and paper mill for textile manufacturing from Bangor Hydro Electric and the Dead River companies. The Striar Textile Mill ran for fifty years; it closed in October 1996, putting an end to almost three hundred jobs. Since

2004, Ayers Island has been owned by Ayers Island LLC, which plans to develop a public accessway via a sculpture garden, nature trails, a canoe and kayak club, an outdoor amphitheater, museum and conference center. The old textile mill still stands on the island and was the ghostly setting for channel VH1's *CelebReality Paranormal Project* in November 2006. Episode 5 starred David Carradine, Mia St. John, Andrew Firestone, Coolio and Bridget Marquardt, and Episode 6 starred Ernie Hudson, Willie Garson, Eric Nies, Courtney Friel and Nicole Eggert. These celebrities spent nights on the island, ghost hunting.

According to VH1, between 1965 and 1975, two hundred four injuries and sixty-three deaths were reported at the Hawthorne Mill on Wobi Island. (The actual names of the mill and island were changed on the Celebreality shows.) The shows states that Samuel Hawthorne built the Hawthorne Mill in the early 1900s on Wobi Island, which apparently had a history of being haunted by the ghost of Wooden Lucy, a native woman cursed with looks that could literally kill. Samuel's young daughter Margaret became obsessed with contacting the spirit of Wooden Lucy in the woods near the mill. One evening, Samuel, startled by something in the woods, swung his shovel in the dark and was horrified to discover he had killed his own daughter. He concealed his crime by dragging her body into the Penobscot River. Legend said Margaret Hawthorne's ghost arose from the water and went to the mill, bent on revenge. When Samuel was found dead in the mill's Records Room, it was believed Margaret's ghost was responsible. However, Margaret and Wooden Lucy's spirits aren't the only ones supposedly haunting the mill. The ghost of mill foreman, John Tanner, joined them after losing an arm to a shredder machine. Allegedly, Tanner had been romantically involved with the wife of the mill's owner, Paul Hawthorne. While his death was reported as an accident, many thought Paul Hawthorne had arranged Tanner's demise.

Much, if not all, of this spine-tingling tale was invented for television entertainment. I was unable to find any records or references of mill-owning Hawthornes in Orono, nor any local stories about Wooden Lucy. Real-life former workers of the Striar Textile Mill may recall a dangerous machine called 'the picker' that mangled and sometimes severed hands and arms – one man died after getting caught in the picker – but he wasn't a foreman, nor was he having an affair with the plant owner's wife.

A terrible disaster did occur in the mill's real history: in October 1892 a pulp digester exploded three hundred feet into the air, killing three mill workers. If any ghost visits this place, it might be one of them.

Ayers Island LLC currently owns the mill and the island. Neither the company president nor the grounds caretaker are willing to discuss the island's ghosts and the two VH1 shows. According to the website at www.ayersisland.com, the island is generally open to the public Monday thru Friday, 9 a.m. to 4:30 p.m.

Gray's Guidelines for Ghost Hunters:

1. Conduct thorough research. Find out as much as you can about a site before you go there. While it may be fun to investigate a site, and then see how your findings stack up with the actual history, it makes more sense to know in advance what (or whom) to look for.

2. Don't drink alcohol or take drugs of any kind prior to or during a ghost hunt. Even cold medicine may muddle your mind and make you less sensitive. On ghost hunts, you want to keep your wits about you.

3. Always tell someone where you're going and when you plan to return. Take care that you tell a trusted soul, not someone bound to play tricks on you.

4. Bring along a buddy. Two or more witnesses can give a more reliable account.

5. Never trespass on private property or on public property that is closed. Not only is it illegal—it can be dangerous as well. Always get permission before entering a posted area. Many graveyards are closed at night because of vandals, so plan your visits during the day. You are responsible for any equipment you leave overnight.

6. Be skeptical and use commonsense. Always look for the logical, non-supernatural explanation.

7. Use your equipment properly. This goes for cameras, video and tape recorders, and sensitive measuring devices as well as psychic aids such as crystals and dowsing rods. (Make certain there is no dust on a camera lens, and don't smoke while snapping a photo!)

8. Leave an area exactly the way you found it. Don't litter. Don't move or remove memorial flowers. Never lean against old tombstones; some are very fragile and may break or topple over.

9. Don't attempt to interfere or fix things. Never try to clean up headstones. It's easy to ruin old stones, especially those that are weathered and crumbling. Unless you know exactly what you're doing, don't try to send a ghost "into the light." What is shown in movies isn't always the case in real life, and it's usually not the case in the afterlife.

10. Respect the ghost you're investigating. If you get startled, try not to scream. Remember, ghosts are people, too, and they probably don't appreciate being screamed at or provoked. Always announce your presence—and don't forget to thank the spirit before you leave.

Glossary

The following section is provided by the Chester County Paranormal Research Society in Pennsylvania and appears in training materials for new investigators. Please visit www.ChesterCountyprs.com for more information.

Air Probe Thermometer
A thermometer with an external probe that is capable of taking instant measurements of the air temperature.

Anomalous field
A field that cannot be explained or ruled out by various possibilities, that can be a representation of spirit or paranormal energy present.

Apparition
A transparent form of a human or animal, a spirit.

Artificial field
A field that is caused by electrical outlets, appliances, etc.

Aural Enhancer
A listening device that enhances or amplifies audio signals. i.e., Orbitor Bionic Ear.

Automatic writing
The act of a spirit guiding a human agent in writing a message that is brought through by the spirit.

Base readings
The readings taken at the start of an investigation and are used as a means of comparing other readings taken later during the course of the investigation.

Demonic Haunting

A haunting that is caused by an inhuman or subhuman energy or spirit.

Dowsing Rods

A pair of L-shaped rods or a single Y-shaped rod, used to detect the presence of what the person using them is trying to find.

Electro-static generator

A device that electrically charges the air often used in paranormal investigations/research as a means to contribute to the materialization of paranormal or spiritual energy.

ELF

Extremely Low Frequency.

ELF Meter/EMF Meter

A device that measures electric and magnetic fields.

EMF

Electro Magnetic Field.

EVP

Electronic Voice Phenomena.

False positive

Something that is being interpreted as paranormal within a picture or video and is, in fact, a natural occurrence or defect of the equipment used.

Gamera

A 35mm film camera connected with a motion detector that is housed in a weatherproof container and takes a picture when movement is detected. Made by Silver Creek Industries.

Geiger Counter

A device that measures gamma and x-ray radiation.

Infra Red

An invisible band of radiation at the lower end of the visible light spectrum. With wavelengths from 750 nm to 1 mm, infrared starts at the end of the microwave spectrum and ends at the beginning of visible light. Infrared transmission typically requires an unobstructed line of sight between transmitter and receiver. Widely used in most audio and video remote controls, infrared transmission is also used for wireless connections between computer devices and a variety of detectors.

Intelligent haunting

A haunting of a spirit or other entity that has the ability to interact with the living and do things that can make its presence known.

Milli-gauss

Unit of measurement, measures in 1000th of a gauss and is named for the famous German mathematician, Karl Gauss.

Orbs

Anomalous spherical shapes that appear on video and still photography.

Pendulum

A pointed item that is hung on the end of a string or chain and is used as a means of contacting spirits. An individual will hold the item and let it hang from the fingertips. The individual will ask questions aloud and the pendulum answers by moving.

Poltergeist haunting

A haunting that has two sides, but same kinds of activity in common. Violent outbursts of activity with doors and windows slamming shut, items being thrown across a room and things being knocked from surfaces. Poltergeist hauntings are usually focused around a specific individual who resides or works at the location of the activity reported, and, in some cases, when the person is not present at the location, activity does not occur. A poltergeist haunting may be the cause of a human agent or spirit/energy that may be present at the location.

Portal

An opening in the realm of the paranormal that is a gateway between one dimension and the next. A passageway for spirits to come and go through. See also Vortex.

Residual haunting

A haunting that is an imprint of an event or person that plays itself out like a loop until the energy that causes it has burned itself out.

Scrying

The act of eliciting information with the use of a pendulum from spirits.

Table Tipping

A form of spirit communication, the act of a table being used as a form of contact. Individuals will sit around a table and lightly place there fingertips on the edge of the table and elicit contact with a spirit. The Spirit will respond by "tipping" or moving the table.

Talking Boards

A board used as a means of communicating with a spirit. Also known as a Quija Board.

Vortex

A place or situation regarded as drawing into its center all that surrounds it.

White Noise

A random noise signal that has the same sound energy level at all frequencies.

EQUIPMENT

In this section, the Chester County Paranormal Research Society looks at the application and benefits of equipment used in investigations with greater detail. The equipment used for an investigation plays a vital role in the ability to collect objective evidence and helps to determine what is and is not paranormal activity. But a key point to be made here is: the investigator is the most important tool on any investigation. With that said, let us now take a look at the main pieces of equipment used during an investigation…

The Geiger Counter

The Geiger counter is device that measures radiation. A "Geiger counter" usually contains a metal tube with a thin metal wire along its middle. The space in between them is sealed off and filled with a suitable gas and with the wire at about +1000 volts relative to the tube.

An ion or electron penetrating the tube (or an electron knocked out of the wall by X-rays or gamma rays) tears electrons off atoms in the gas. Because of the high positive voltage of the central wire, those electrons are then attracted to it. They gain energy that collide with atoms and release more electrons, until the process snowballs into an "avalanche", producing an easily detectable pulse of current. With a suitable filling gas, the flow of electricity stops by itself, or else the electrical circuitry can help stop it.

The instrument was called a "counter" because every particle passing it produced an identical pulse, allowing particles to be counted, usually electronically. But it did not tell anything about their identity or energy, except that they must have sufficient energy to penetrate the walls of the counter.

The Geiger counter is used in paranormal research to measure the background radiation at a location. The working theory in this field is that paranormal activity can effect the background radiation. In some cases, it will increase the radiation levels and in other cases it will decrease the levels.

Digital and 35mm Film Cameras

The camera is an imperative piece of equipment that enabled us to gather objective evidence during a case. Some of the best evidence presented from cases of paranormal activity over the years has been because of photographs taken. If you own your own digital camera or 35mm film camera, you need to be fully aware of what the cameras abilities and limitations are. Digital cameras have been at the center of great debate in the field of paranormal research over the years.

The earlier incarnations of digital cameras were full of inherent problems and notorious for creating "false positive" pictures. A "false positive" picture is a picture that has anomalous elements within the picture that are the result of a camera defect or other natural occurrence. There are many pictures scattered about the internet that claim to be of true paranormal activity, but in fact they are "false positives." Orbs, defined as anomalous paranormal energy that can show up as balls of light or streaks in still photography or video, are the most controversial pictures of paranormal energy in the field. There are so many theories (good and bad) about the origin of orbs and what they are. Every picture in the CCPRS collection that has an orb—or orbs—are not presented in a way that state that they are absolutely paranormal of nature. I have yet to capture an orb photo that made me feel certain that in fact it is of a paranormal nature.

If you use your own camera, understand that your camera is vital. I encourage all members who own their own cameras to do research on the make and model of the camera and see what other consumers are saying about them. Does the manufacturer give any info regarding possible defects or design flaws with that particular model? Understanding your camera will help to rule out the possibility of interpreting a "false positive" for an authentic picture of paranormal activity.

Video Cameras

The video camera is also a fundamental tool in the investigation as another way for collecting objective evidence that can support the proof of paranormal activity. The video camera can be used in various ways during the investigation. It can be set on a tripod and left in a location where paranormal activity has been reported. It can also be used as a hand-held camera and the investigator will take it with them during their walk through investigation as a means of documenting to hopefully capture anomalous activity on tape. Infrared technology has become a feature on most consumer-level video cameras and depending on the manufacturer can be called "night shot" or "night alive." What this technology does is allow us to use the camera in zero light. Most cameras with this feature will add a green tint or haze to the camera when it is being used in this mode. A video camera with this ability holds great appeal to the paranormal investigator.

EMF/ELF Meters

EMF=Electro Magnetic Frequency ELF=Extremely Low Frequency

What is an EMF/ELF meter? Good question. The EMF/ELF meter is a meter that measures Electric and Magnetic fields in an AC or DC current field. It measures in a unit of measurement called "milligauss," named for the famous German mathematician, Karl Gauss. Most meters will measure in a range of 1-5 or 1-10 milli-gauss.

The reason that EMF meters are used in paranormal research is because of the theory that a spirit or paranormal energy can add to the energy field when it is materializing or is present in a location. The theory says that, typically, an energy that measures between 3-7 milli-gauss may be of a paranormal origin. This doesn't mean that an artificial field can't also measure within this range. That is why we take base readings and make maps notating where artificial fields occur. The artificial fields are a direct result of electricity, i.e. wiring, appliances, light switches, electrical outlets, circuit breakers, high voltage power lines, sub-stations, etc.

The Earth emits a naturally occurring magnetic field all around us and has an effect on paranormal activity. Geo-magnetic storm activity can also have a great influence on paranormal activity. For more information on this kind of phenomena visit: www.noaa.sec. com.

There are many different types of EMF meters; and each one, although it measures with the same unit of measurement, may react differently. An EMF meter can range from anywhere from $12 to $1,000 or more depending on the quality and features that it has. Most meters are measuring the AC (alternating current, the type of fields created by man-made electricity) fields and some can measure DC (direct current-naturally occurring fields, batteries also fall into the category of DC) fields. The benefit of having a meter that can measure DC fields is that they will automatically filter out the artificial fields created by AC fields and can pick up more naturally occurring electro magnetic fields. Some of the higher-tech EMF meters are so sensitive that they can pick up the fields generated by living beings. The EMF meter was originally designed to measure the earth's magnetic fields and also to measure the fields created by electrical an artificial means.

There have been various studies over the years about the long-term effects of individuals living in or near high fields. There has been much controversy as to whether or not long term exposure to high fields can lead to cancer. It has been proven though that no matter what, long-term exposure to high fields can be harmful to your health. The ability to locate these high fields within a private residence or business is vital to the investigation. We may offer suggestions to the client as to possible solutions for dealing with high fields. The wiring in a home or business can greatly affect the possibility of high fields. If the wiring is old and/or not shielded correctly, it can emit high fields that may affect the ability to correctly notate any anomalous fields that may be present.

Audio Recording Equipment

Audio recording equipment is used for conducting EVP (Electronic Voice Phenomena) research and experiments. What is an EVP? An EVP is a phenomenon where paranormal voices or sounds can be captured with audio recording devices. The theory is that the activity will imprint directly onto the device or tape, but has not been proven to be an absolute fact. The use of an external microphone is essential when conducting EVP experiments with analog recording equipment. The internal microphone on an analog tape recorder can pick up the background noise of the working parts within the tape recorder and can taint the evidence as a whole. Most digital recorders are quiet enough to use the internal microphone, but as a general rule of thumb, we do not use them. An external microphone will be used always. Another theory about EVP research is that an authentic EVP will happen within the range 250-400hz. This is a lower frequency range and isn't easily heard by the human ear, and the human voice does not emit in this range. EVP is rarely heard at the moment it happens—it is usually revealed during the playback and analysis portion of the investigation.

Thermometers

The use of a thermometer in an investigation goes without saying. This is how we monitor the temperature changes during the course of an investigation. CCPRS is currently using Digital thermometers with remote sensors as a way to set up a perimeter and to notate any changes in a stationary location of an investigation. The Air-probe thermometer can take "real time" readings that are instantly accurate. This is the more appropriate thermometer for measuring air temperature and "cold spots" that may be caused by the presence of paranormal phenomena. The IR Non-contact thermometer is the most misused thermometer in the field of paranormal research. CCPRS does not own or use IR Non-contact thermometers for this reason. The IR (infrared) Non-contact thermometer is meant for measuring surface temperatures from a remote location. It shoots an infrared beam out to an object and bounces to the unit and gives the temperature reading. I have seen, first hand, investigators using this thermometer as a way to measure air temperature. NO, this is not correct! Enough said. In an email conversation that I have had with Grant Wilson from TAPS, he has said that, "Any change in temperature that can't be measured with your hand is not worth notating…"

Sources

"A Haunted Farm and Architectural Beauty," *The Lincoln County News*, Vol. 132, No.5, Sept. 7, 2005.

Amstead, Alicia. "New Venue's Goal: to be a Favorite Haunt, Ex-mortuary gets new life as Winterport restaurant," *Bangor Daily News*, Dec. 20, 2006.

Ariel. *Strange and Unusual Stories, Vols. I & II*. Stories of Maine, Ariel Productions, audiocassette, 1992.

Baker, Scott, "Tales from Evergreen: Mary Jane Emerson Clapp," AroundMaine. com, October 15, 2003.

Baker, William, "The Captains Remember," *200 Years of Lubec History 1776-1976*, Lubec, Maine: Lubec Historical Society, 1976.

Ballard, Martha Moore, from her diaries written in Hallowell, Maine, 1806.

Bantry, John. "Secret of 50-Year-Old Murder Case - Amazing Maine Mystery Cleared Up - Real Truth Astounding in Its Strange Angles," *Rockland Courier-Gazette*, Sept. 8, 1930.

Barron, Maria & Smallwood, Terri. Calendar page, Metamorphosis, Vol. 2, No. 7, July 2003.

Bartlett, Gately. Road Anomalies Tour (RAT), 2000, www.ratrun.com/maine.htm.

Beck, Robin, "Meet Jim and Gerry Botti, New Owners of the Kenniston Hill Inn," *Boothbay Register*, Vol. 124, No. 29, July 20, 2000.

Belkin, Douglas, "Is Anyone There?", *The Boston Globe*, Oct. 23, 2005.

Bell, Tom, "Presumpscot River: Sebago Lake to Westbrook," *MaineToday*, Aug. 26, 2001.

Benoit, Peter. *History of Jewell Island, Maine*. Wasilla, Alaska: self-published, 1996.

Blackington, Alton Hall. "Cling-Clang The Vaulting Peddler," *Mysterious New England*. Edited by Austin M. Stevens. Dublin, New Hampshire: Yankee Publishing, Inc., 1971.

Blanchard, Fessenden S. *Ghost Towns of New England: Their ups and downs*. New York, New York: Dodd, Mead & Co., 1960.

Bolte, Mary. *Haunted New England: A Devilish View of the Yankee Past*. Riverside, Connecticut: Chatham Press, 1972.

Branen, Alyssa, "Hauntings in Maine: Ghosties of the Pine Tree State," AC Associated Content The People's Media Company, www.associatedcontent.com, Nov. 29, 2006.

Brewer, Rod, "Cry of the Lost Hunter," www.Whistlesmith.com, Dec. 8, 2006.

Bruce, Noah. "Who's Buried in Longfellow's Tomb and Other Mysteries Beyond the Grave," *Portland Phoenix*, Portland, Maine, Oct. 25, 2001.

Cahill, Robert Ellis. *Lighthouse Mysteries of the North Atlantic*. Danvers, Massachusetts: Old Saltbox Publishing Co., 1998.

New England's Ghostly Haunts. Peabody, Massachusetts: Chandler-Smith Publishing House, Inc., 1983.

Caldwell, Bill. *Islands of Maine: Where America Really Began*. Camden, Maine: Down East Books, 1981.

Captain D, Daytripping, Area Attractions Bangor/Brewer Towards Ellsworth, Captain D's Downeast Directory of the Unique: www.captaind.com.

Carter, Bruce. *Oblivion & Dead Relatives Downeast*. Ellsworth, Maine: Downeast Graphics & Printing, 1996

Casey, Maura J. "The Little Desert That Grew in Maine," *The New York Times*. New York City, New York: The New York Times Co., Sept. 22, 2006.

Castner, Harold W. "Was She Buried Alive?" *Mysterious New England*. Edited by Austin M. Stevens. Dublin, New Hampshire: Yankee Publishing, Inc., 1971.

Celebrity Paranormal Project, Episodes 5 & 6, Los Angeles, California: 51 Minds Entertainment, produced by VH1, aired Nov. 22, 2006 & Nov. 26, 2006.

Chmelecki, Lisa. "Ghost-hunting Couple Photograph their Findings," *Portsmouth Herald*. Portsmouth, New Hampshire: Seacoast Media Group, Jan. 7, 2001.

Citro, Joseph A. and Foulds, Diane. *Curious New England - The Unconventional Traveler's Guide to Eccentric Destinations*. Lebanon, New Hampshire: University Press of New England, 2003.

Cursed in New England - Stories of Damned Yankees. Guilford, Connecticut: The Globe Pequot Press, 2004.

Passing Strange: True Tales of New England Hauntings and Horrors. New York, New York: Houghton Mifflin Company, 1997.

Weird New England - Your Travel Guide to New England's Local Legends and Best Kept Secrets. New York, New York: Sterling Publishing Company, 2005.

Connell, Sarah. *Bates College Off the Record*. Pittsburgh, Pennsylvania: College Prowler, Inc., 2006.

Cook, Rita. "The Ghosts of Bethel, Maine," *The Heart of New England*. Marcia Passos Duffy, Publisher. www.theheartofnewengland.com

Cornish, Paul and Hedy. "The Curse of Mollyockett," www.riverrestaurant.com, 1998.

Curtis, Abigail, "We've Got Spirit - First Psychic and Paranormal Festival Draws Hundreds of Visitors to Fort Knox," *Bangor Daily News*, July 4, 2005.

D'Entremont, Jeremy. "Cape Neddick "Nubble" Light," York, Maine: www.lighthouse.cc/capeneddick/history.html, January 6, 2007.

Dandurant, Karen. "Ghostly Tale," *The York Weekly*. York, Maine: October 29, 2003.

"Hauntings and Spooky Tales of York Survive from the 1600s," *Portsmouth Herald*. Portsmouth, New Hampshire: Seacoast Media Group, October 25, 2003.

de Costa, Benjamin Franklin Dr. *Northmen in Maine*. Albany, New York: Joel Munsell, 1870.

Dean, Jaspar. *A Narrative of the Shipwreck of the Nottingham-Galley*. London, England: R. Tookey, publisher; 1762 (5th ed.).

Delaware County Paranormal Research, "High Point near Belfast, Maine," www.delcoghosts.com.

Desert of Maine website: www.desertofmaine.com.

DeWire, Elinor. Guardians of the Light: Stories of U.S. Lighthouse Keepers. Sarasota, Florida: Pineapple Press, 1995.

"Discover the Wonder of the Oxford Hills," Letterboxing Project, May-September 2006.

Dorson, Richard Mercer. *Buying the Wind: Regional Folklore in the United States*. Chicago, Illinois: University of Chicago Press, 1916.

Dorson, Richard Mercer. "Jonathan Draws the Long Bow," Lewiston Journal: Nov. 1, 1938.

Downer, Deborah, editor. *Classic American Ghost Stories*. Atlanta, Georgia: August House, 1990.

'Dr. Moses Mason and His House,' Sunday River On-Line USA: www.Net2Market.com.

Drake, Samuel Adams. *Nooks and Corners of the New England Coast*. New York, New York: Harper & Brothers, 1875.

Drake, Samuel Adams. *The Pine Tree Coast*. Boston, Massachusetts: Estes & Lauriet, 1890.

Dunton, Alvin. *The True Story of the Hart-Meservey Murder Trial*. Boston, Massachusetts: self-published, 1882.

Eaton, Cyrus, A.M. *Annals of the Town of Warren; with an Early History of St. George's, Broad Bay and the Neighboring Settlements on the Waldo Patent*. Hallowell, Maine: Masters, Smith & Company, 1851.

Edes, Peter. "Horrid Murder. Augusta (Kennebec) July 11," Kennebec Gazette: July 14, 1806

Elwell, Edward Henry. *Fraternity Papers*. Portland, Maine: James S. Staples, Printer, 1886.

Ernest, Dagney C. "Hauntings in Maine's Midcoast," Steppin' Out: Your Guide To Life In Coastal Maine. www.steppinoutmaine.com, Oct. 23, 2002.

Faria, Glenn M. "The Ledgelawn Inn 1904," *Reasons to Write*. Hyannis, Cape Cod, Massachusetts: Michael Patrick Tourism Communications, Ltd., 2000.

Federal Writers' Project. Maine, A Guide "Down East." Boston, Massachusetts, 1937.

Fedler, Fred. *Media Hoaxes*. Ames, Iowa: Iowa State University Press, 1989.

Fernia, Michael. 'Putting the Vice in Vice President,' Bunkosquad. Boston, Massachusetts: www.bunkosquad.com, Feb. 17, 2006

Ferriss, Lloyd. "The Idol's Curse," Maine Sunday Telegram. Portland, Maine: Blethen Maine Newspapers, Inc., Seattle Times Company, November 29, 1987 (updated by Watson, Meryl J.).

Fish, Jen. "Stage Fright," *Maine Today*. Portland, Maine: Blethen Maine Newspapers, Seattle Times Company, Oct. 30, 2002.

Fletcher, Kim. "A Ghost Story," *The Lincoln County News*, Vol. 132, No. 5, Oct. 12, 2005.

Folsom, George. *The History of Saco and Biddeford*. Saco, Maine: Alex C. Putnam, 1830 (Somersworth, New Hampshire: New Hampshire Publishing Company, 1975).

Fort William Henry: www.forttours.com

Friends of Colonial Pemaquid New Harbor, Maine, 'History, Museum,' 2001.

Friends of Cumston Hall, The Centennial Project Overview: www.cumstonhall. org.

Friends of Sequin Island, Fall 2005 newsletter.

"Ghost Hunt," *The Maine Campus Online*. Boston, Massachusetts: College Publisher, November 3, 2003.

'girlawhirl chills out in bar harbor maine,' www.Girlawhirl.com, Sept. 1, 2006.

Goodman, Giselle. "Beautiful but cruel, the Saco reveals her many moods," *Maine Today Outdoors*. Portland, Maine: Blethen Maine Newspapers, Inc., August 14, 2002.

Goold, William. *Portland in the Past with Historical Notes of Old Falmouth*. Portland, Maine: B. Thurston & Company, 1886.

Gosling, Nick. "Bucksport Librarian Takes on Unsolved Murder," *The Ellsworth American*. Ellsworth, Maine:published in-house, Feb. 1, 2007.

"Gravesite of Purrin(g)ton Family Found," *Kennebec Current*, Kennebec Historical Society, May-June 2006.

Greene, Francis Byron. *History of Boothbay, Southport and Boothbay Harbor, Maine. 1623-1905: With Family Genealogies*. Portland, Maine: Loring, Short & Harmon, 1906.

Griffin, Chip. *Damariscove: First Maypole Celebration in America*. www.griffinlawoffices.com/DAMARISCOVE-First_Maypole.pdf, May 1, 2003

Hahn, Natalie White. *A History of Winter Harbor Maine*. self-published, 1974.

Haines, Max. *50 Headline-Grabbing Murders From Around The World*. New York, New York: Barnes & Noble Books, 2005.

Hallet, Richard. "Saco River Outlives Indian Curse," *Maine Sunday Telegram*, June 29, 1947.

Hansen, Gunnar. "The Unfinished Flight of the White Bird," *Mysteries, Marvels & Nightmares: More than 40 Exciting Stories from the Pages of Yankee Magazine*. Dublin, New Hampshire: Yankee Books, 1987.

Harrington, George Leavitt. "Classified Sanitarium Directory of Eastern United States." Brooklyn, New York: Brooklyn Medical Journal, 1906.

'Haunted Locations of Maine,' The Mystery Network: www.mysterykingdoms.com

Hawthorne, Nathaniel. *Passages from the American Note Books*. Edited by Sophia Hawthorne. Cambridge, Massachusetts: Bigelow and Company, 1868.

Hewitt, Rich. "Calling All Ghosts: Fort Knox Spirits Invited to Contact Bangor Twosome," *Bangor Daily News*, August 9, 2004.

Hewitt, Rich. "Mystery Stone Unearthed at Fort Knox - Granite Slab Hints at Site's History," *Bangor Daily News*, April 18, 2005

"Psychics to Call Spirits at Fort Knox," *Bangor Daily News*, June 24, 2005

Hiatt, J.M. and Moye, W. Stephans, "Ghosts of the Air," *100 Little Ghastly Ghost Stories*. Selected by Stefan Dziemianowicz, Robert H. Weinberg & Martin H. Greenberg. New York, New York: Sterling Publishing Co., Inc., 2003.

History Channel's The Cold Spot Documentaries: Haunted History: Maine, A&E Television Networks, New York, New York: New Video, 2000.

"History of Cumston Hall," Cumston Public Library, July 30, 1997.

History's Mysteries: Ghost Ships, Episode 11, The History Channel, A&E Television Networks, New York, New York: A&E Home Video, 1995.

Hontvet, Maren. "Murder Testimony of Maren Hontvet," June 1873 transcript, www.SeacoastNH.com, 2006.

Howe, David Wait and Howe, Gilman Bigelow. *John Howe Genealogy*. self-published, 1929.

Hughes, Pat. "Flagstaff, Maine: The Wet Ghost Town," *There was a Land by Former Residents & Friends of the Dead River Valley*. Farmington, Maine: Knowlton & McLeary, 1999.

Jart, Chris. "Was Hannibal Hamlin a Zombie?" www.StrangeMaine.com, Feb. 16, 2006.

Jasper, Mark. *Haunted Inns of New England*. Yarmouth Port, Massachusetts: On Cape Publications, 2000.

Jayz Ghost Stories from the Eastern United States website: http://members.tripod.com/jayboy74.

Jewett, Sarah Orne. "The Old Town of Berwick," *The New England Magazine*. Boston, Massachusetts, 1894 (Berwick, Maine: The Old Berwick Historical Society, 1967).

Johnson, Lelia A. Clark. *Sullivan & Sorrento Since 1760*. Ellsworth, Maine: Hancock County Publishing Co., 1953.

Kenderdine, Muriel. "Cast & Crew," Issue No. 85, Portland, Maine, August 2005.

Kimball, Michael. "Searching for Voices from the Other Side," *Yankee Magazine*, No. 11. Dublin, New Hampshire: Yankee Publishing, Inc., Nov. 1984.

Klein, Barbro Sklute. *Legends and Folk Beliefs in a Swedish American Community*. Manchester, New Hampshire: Ayer Company Publishers, 1980.

Kristoff, Lisa. "Channel 7's Night at the Opera House," *Boothbay Register*, Vol. 128, No. 9, Oct. 6, 2005.

"Ghost Hunters United Revisits the Opera House," *Boothbay Register*, Vol. 129, No. 45, Nov. 9, 2006.

"Haunted: The Welch House Inn," *Boothbay Register*, Vol. 129, No. 43, Oct. 26, 2006.

Labbe, Rod. "Familiars & Haunts," *Maine Today Morning Sentinal*, Oct. 29, 2006.

Lecompte, Nancy. *Last of the Androscoggins, Molly Ockett, Abenaki Healing Woman*. Lewiston, Maine: Ne-Do-Ba, 1997.

Left Field - Paranormal Studies & Investigations: www.leftfield-psi.net/ghosts/haunted places

Lodi, Edward. *A Gathering of New England Ghosts*. Middleborough, Massachusetts: Rock Village Publishing, 2001.

Loring, Rev. Amasa. *A History of Shapleigh, Maine*. self-published, 1854.

"Lucerne Inn: The Heart of Dedham's History," Our Town Section, *The Ellsworth American*. Ellsworth, Maine, 2002.

Lydia Carver Story, 2005, Inn By The Sea website: http://www.innbythesea.com/carver/

Maine State Archives; Maine DOT Section 4(f) Statement to Supplement the Environmental Assessment for Improvements to a Section of Route 26 in the Towns of New Gloucester and Poland, Maine, August 1998, Appendix A.

Mayne, Marti. "Great Places To Sleep With A Ghost," BedandBreakfast.com's *Annual 2005 Round-up of Bootiful Places and Spooky Faces*, Press Release: 'Sleep With A Ghost On The Coast This Halloween,' Historic Inns of Rockland: www.historicinnsofrockland.com/specials/halloween.

Michaud, Kelly, editor. *Get Your Spook On,' Steppin' Out - Your Guide To Life In Coastal Maine*. Rockland, Maine: Courier Publications, 2004.

Millburg, Steve & Walling, Mamie. "Top 10 Haunted Lighthouses," *Coastal Living Magazine*. Birmingham, Alabama: October 2006.

Miller, Aaron C. "Ghostly Stories in Wiscasset," *Wiscasset Newspaper*, Vol. 30, No. 43, Oct. 28, 1999.

Monks, Sheryl. *Ghostly Lighthouses from Maine to Florida*. Winston-Salem, North Carolina: John F. Blair Publisher, 2005.

Monroe, Judith W. *Peripheral Visions Ghost Stories from Swans Island, Maine*. Durham, North Carolina: Crone's Own Press, 1992.

Moran, Mark & Sceurman, Mark. *Weird U.S.: Your Travel Guide to America's Local Legends And Best Kept Secrets*. New York City, New York: Barnes & Noble: Sterling Publishing Co., Inc., 2004.

Munn, Charles Clark. *Uncle Terry: A Story of the Maine Coast*. Boston, Massachusetts: Lee and Shepard, 1900.

Murchison, D. "Haunted Places Report," *The Hauck Report Monthly Newsletter*, Vol. 2, No. 5, May 1999.

Murphy, Edward D. "Ghost Hunters", *MaineToday*. Portland, Maine: Blethen Maine Newspapers, Seattle Times Co., October 2003.

Noddin, Peter. "Phantom Crashes Maine's Worst Aircraft Disasters That Never Happened!" Bangor, Maine: Maine Aviation Historical Society, June 2000.

Norman, Michael, & Scott, Beth. *Historic Haunted America*. New York, New York: Tor/Forge, 2006.

Norton, Mary Beth. *In the Devil's Snare - The Salem Witchcraft Crisis of 1692*. New York, New York: Knopf, 2002.

O'Brien, Rose. "Ghost Lady of Hendricks Head," *Lewiston Journal*, July 14, 1956

Ochterbeck, Cynthia Clayton. *Michelin Green Guide: New England*. South Greenville, South Carolina: Michelin Travel Publications, 6th Edition, 1993

Original Tales True Stories by Real People: www.original tales.com, Feb. 25, 2005

Pacy, Brooke. "The Man Who Saved Wreck Island," *The Lincoln County News*, Vol. 132, No. 5, Sept. 7, 2005.

Paper, Henry. "Portland's Famous Ghost Stories." *Greater Portland*, Issue 30, No. 5, Fall 1985.

Peavey, Elizabeth. "Natural Born Innkeeper," *Downeast Magazine*, April 1997.

Poland, Maine. "Maine Unusual Hometown Attractions": www.yourhometown. org.

"Poland Spring Inn, The Ultimate Collection of the Strange": www.StrangeUSA. com

Poland Spring Preservation Society, "History of Poland Spring": www.polandspringps. org/history.

Potter, Gail M. "The Legend of Handkerchief Moody,'" *Mysterious New England*. Edited by Austin M. Stevens. Dublin, New Hampshire: Yankee Publishing, Inc., 1971.

Pullen, John J. *Joshua Chamberlain: A Hero's Life and Legacy*. Mechanicsburg, Pennsylvania: Stackpole Books, 1999.

Pulsifer, Joshua D. "Trial of George Knight of Poland, for murder: before the Supreme Judicial Court of Maine at Auburn, Androscoggin County, commencing Feb. 16, 1857," *The Lewiston Falls Journal*. Lewiston, Maine: Waldron & Dingley, 1857

Rayno, Terry. "A Whole New Way of Life," *Plymouth Magazine*, Vol. XX, No. 2, Winter 2005.

Reaves, Tony. "Orono's Celebrity Ghost Hunt," *The Maine Campus*. University of Maine in Orono: College Publisher Network, Dec. 11, 2006

Reid, Harvey, 2001-2002 Harvey Reid Newsletter, York, Maine

Ritchie, Susan, Rev. Sermon: "The Larger Hope: Life Without Fear," Dublin Unitarian Universalist Church, www.nuuc.org/sermon/sermon960929.html. Columbus, Ohio, Sept. 29, 1996

Robbins, Ryan R. "The Brady Gang," *Bangor in Focus*, www.bangorinfo.com. "Thomas Hill Standpipe," *Bangor in Focus*, www. bangorinfo.com.

Roberts, Kenneth. *Boon Island Including Contemporary Accounts of the Wreck of the Nottingham Galley*. Edited by Jack Bales & Richard Warner, reprint Hanover, New Hampshire: University Press of New England, 1996. (New York, New York: Doubleday, 1956).

Robicheau, Leanne M. "Haunted Memories - Keepers of Owls Head Light tell tales of ghosts in their beds, plastic pumpkins that move by themselves," *Bangor Daily News*, Oct. 31, 2006.

Rogers, Richard P., director. "A Midwife's Tale—Eighteenth Century America Through a Woman's Eyes," The American Experience. PBS Documentary, 1998.

Rolde, Neil. *So You Think You Know Maine*. Gardiner, Maine: Tilbury House Publishers, 1st Edition, 1984.

Rothwell, Hella. "The Captain Lord Mansion." Carmel, California: Travel Press Kit.

Rumsey, Barbara. "The Baby That Washed Ashore at Hendricks Head, Parts I & II," *Out of Our Past, Stories of Hendricks Head Light*. Boothbay Region Historical Society.

Sargent, Colin. "Ghosts R Us," Portland Monthly, summer guide 2004.

SB-ME-2006-53998: Blackwoods Scenic Byway Planning and Management, Maine Department of Transportation.

Scarborough, Dorothy. *Humorous Ghost Stories*. New York & London: G.P. Putnam's Sons, Knickerbocker Press, 1921.

Scary New England: www.angelfire.com/scary/newengland

Schulte, Carol Olivieri. *Ghosts on the Coast of Maine*. Camden, Maine: Down East Books, 1989 (reprint 1996).

Sell, Shawn. "10 Great Places to Haunt a Ghost Town," *USA Today*. McLean, Virginia: Gannett Co., Oct. 21, 2005.

Seymour, Tom. *Tom Seymour's Maine: A Maine Anthology*, Lincoln, Nebraska: iUniverse, 2003.

Shields, Tom. "Ghosts Don't Spook Down East Couple," *Bangor Daily News*, August 6-7, 1983.

Shore Village Museum Newsletter #1-97, Rockland, Maine, Apr. 8, 1997

"SHOT ANOTHER, THEN HIMSELF, The Story of the Murder and Suicide on Wood Island," *Biddeford Daily Journal*, June 2, 1896.

Sicard, Cheri. "The Ghosts of Waldo County," *Weird Wanderings*. www.FabulousTravel.com

Skinner, Charles M. *Myths and Legends in Our Own Land, Vol. 1*. Boston, Massachusetts: Adamant Media Corporation, Elibron Classics, reprint 2001 (Philadelphia & London: J.B. Lippincott Company, 1896).

Snow, Edward Rowe. "Baby That Washed Ashore," *Famous Lighthouses of New England*. Dublin, New Hampshire: Yankee Publishing, Inc., 1945.

Souliere, Michelle. "Finding Strange Maine," *Lewiston Sun Journal*, Sept. 3, 2006
"Hiram Haunted Road Legend," www.StrangeMaine, January 24, 2007
"Purrington Massacre Update," www.StrangeMaine.com, July 31, 2006.

Stack, Robert (host). Unsolved Mysteries: Mysterious Legends Episode 24. Burbank, California: Cosgrove/Meurer Productions, Burbank, California, May 3, 1989.

Stansfield, Charles A. Jr. Haunted Maine: Ghosts and Strange Phenomena of the Pine Tree State. Mechanicsburg, Pennsylvania: Stackpole Books, 2007.

Stanwood, Chief. "Cling Clang," *The Ellsworth American*, Oct. 1, 1947.

Steitz, George C., director. Cold Spot Documentaries: Haunted Lighthouses, The Learning Channel, Discovery TLC, October 1998.

Stevens, C.J. *The Supernatural Side of Maine*. Phillips, Maine: John Wade, Publisher, 2002.

Stevens, John Austin. "The Story of Castine, Maine," *The Magazine of American History with Notes and Queries*, compiled by William Abbatt. New York, New York: A.S. Barnes Publishing Co., 1893.

Stevens, William Oliver. *Unbidden Guests: A Book of Real Ghosts*. New York, New York: Dodd, Mead & Co., 1945.

Sylvester, Herbert Milton. *Indian Wars of New England*. Cleveland, Ohio: Arthur H. Clark Company, 1910.
Maine Pioneer Settlements. Boston, Massachusetts: W.B. Clarke publishing, 1909.

Teehan, M. F. *Standard Hospital Asylum and Institution Directory*. Marshall, Missouri: Standard Publishing Company, 1921.

Thaxter, Celia Laughton. *Among the Isles of Shoals*. East Lansing, Michigan: Scholarly Publishing Office, University of Michigan Library, reprint 2005 (Boston, Massachusetts: Houghton Mifflin Company, 1893).

Thaxter, Celia Laughton. "A Memorable Murder," *Atlantic Monthly*. Boston, Massachusetts: May 1875.

"The Day Machine Gun Fire Rattled Bangor," *Bangor Daily News*. (History Celebrating 100 Years of the Bangor Daily News), June 17-18, 1989 (Original headline: 'Al Brady and Partner Gunned Down,' Bangor Daily News, Oct. 12, 1937).

"The Drummer Boy of Castine — A Ghost Story," *The Wilson Museum Bulletin*, Vol. 2, No. 22, Castine Scientific Society, Fall 1981.

Thompson, Ryan. "Woolwich Couple to Open Restaurant," *Wiscasset Newspaper*, Vol. 37, No. 10, March 9, 2006.

Thompson, William O. "Maine Ghosts: The Dead Still Whisper." Directed by Don Moore. Lewiston, Maine: Video Services Unlimited, 1992.

Taylor, Troy. "Ghosts of Portland," Ghosts of the Prairie, Haunted Maine: www.prairieghosts.com/portland

Ulrich, Laurel Thatcher. *A Midwife's Tale: The Life of Martha Ballard based on her diary, 1785–1812*. New York, New York: Vintage Books, Random House, 1991.

Varney, George J. *A Gazetteer of the State of Maine*. Boston, Massachusetts: B.B. Russell Publishing, 1886.

Verde, Thomas A. *Maine Ghosts & Legends: 26 Encounters with the Supernatural*. Camden, Maine: Down East Books, 1989.

Voight, Peggy. "150 Share Stories, Memories At "Damariscove Remembered",' *Boothbay Register*, Vol. 30, No. 4, Jan. 25, 2007.

Walls, Melissa. "Criterion tours offer trip back in time," *The Mount Desert Islander*, June 23, 2006.

"Was it Wagner's? Dagger Found in House Where Murderer Used to Live," *Portsmouth Herald*, Feb. 4, 1904.

Washuk, Bonnie. "Ghost in the Governor's Office," *Lewiston Sun Journal*, April 26, 2004.

Webster, Elizabeth B. "Developers Don't Let Curse Bother Them," *Maine Today*, Dec. 19, 2003.

Wheeler, George Augustus, A.M.M.D. *History of Castine, Penobscot, and Brooksville, Maine; Including the Ancient Settlement of Pentagöet*. Bangor, Maine: Burr & Robinson, 1875.

"White Bird," NUMA (National Underwater and Marine Agency) newsletter, October 1984.

Whittier, John Greenleaf. "Funeral Tree of the Sokokis," *The Complete Works of John Greenleaf Whittier, Volume 1, Native and Legendary Poems*. Kila, Montana: Kessinger Publishing, 2004.

WiccanRoad: The Poland Spring Inn, Ghost Stories, Maine: www.wiccanroad. com

Wiggins, Bill. "Mystery of the White Bird," *LookSmart Air Classics*, July 1999

Williams, Katherine. "Gouldsboro, 'For Rent: One Lighthouse Cottage," *The Ellsworth American*, Aug. 1, 2002.

Williams, Yona. *Haunted Lighthouses: Michigan, Maine & Florida*, www.unexplainable.net, March 14, 2006

Haunted Maine: Brunswick, Rockport & More. Unexplainable.net, March 28, 2006

Wintersteel, Haunted Places: www.wintersteel.com

Wood, Cyndi. "Prospect Harbor Light: A History with Ghosts," *The Ellsworth American & Mount Desert Islander*, August 2006.

Woodbury, Charles Levi. *The Woodbury Family*. Manchester, New Hampshire: John B. Clarke Company, 1904.

Woodlawn Museum: www.woodlawnmuseum.com

www.familyviolenceproject.org, 2006 newsletter

Index